CANDLESTICK CHARTING
EXPLAINED
WORKBOOK

CANDLESTICK CHARTING
EXPLAINED
WORKBOOK

Step-by-Step Exercises

and Tests

to Help You Master Candlestick Charting

Gregory L. Morris

The McGraw·Hill Companies

10 11 12 13 14 15 QVS/QVS 22 21 20 19 18

ISBN 978-0-07-174221-4
MHID 0-07-174221-2
e-ISBN 978-0-07-174646-5
e-MHID 978-0-07-174646-3

This publication is designed to provide accurate and authoritative information in regard to the subject matter covered. It is sold with the understanding that neither the author nor the publisher is engaged in rendering legal, accounting, securities trading, or other professional services. If legal advice or other expert assistance is required, the services of a competent professional person should be sought.
—*From a Declaration of Principles Jointly Adopted by a Committee of the American Bar Association and a Committee of Publishers and Associations*

Library of Congress Cataloging-in-Publication Data
Morris, Gregory L.
Candlestick charting explained workbook: step-by-step exercises and tests to help you master candlestick charting / by Gregory Morris. -- 1st ed.
p. cm.
Includes index.
ISBN-13: 978-0-07-174221-4 (alk. paper)
ISBN-10: 0-07-174221-2 (alk. paper)
1. Stocks--Charts, diagrams, etc. 2. Stocks--Prices--Charts, diagrams, etc. 3. Stock price forecasting. 4. Stocks--Prices--Japan--Charts, diagrams, etc. I. Title.
HG4638.M676 2012
332.63'2042--dc23   2011036541

McGraw-Hill products are available at special quantity discounts to use as premiums and sales promotions or for use in corporate training programs. To contact a representative, please e-mail us at bulksales@mcgraw-hill.com.

This book is printed on acid-free paper.

To

Laura

CONTENTS

Preface   ix

Acknowledgments   xi

1

Enlistment: Getting Ready for Duty   1

2

The Foundation: Preparing for Battle   9

3

Reversal Patterns: Repelling the Advance   17

4

Continuation Patterns: The Next Attack Wave   73

5

Intelligence Briefing: Pattern Identification and Filtering   97

6

Honorable Discharge: Putting It All Together   131

Appendix A: Other Japanese Charting Methods   147

Appendix B: Academic Papers on Candlesticks   149

Sources   151

Answer Key   155

Index   157

PREFACE

After writing the third edition to *Candlestick Charting Explained* in 2006, I thought my candlestick writing days were over. Not so fast! After giving hundreds of lectures and presentations on the subject, I found that even though the book was quite thorough, many people still needed the academic approach to assist in their learning process. Moreover, I continue to witness a terrible misunderstanding about what candlesticks can offer a trader. I think this is so because some authors tend to overpromote their books and software, offering quick solutions to wealth. I don't even want to go there with an opinion on what I think of that approach. There is no magic in candlesticks, there is no ancient wisdom to glean, and there is nothing in candlesticks that you could not get from bar charts. Candlesticks just make it easier and certainly more visually appealing. Hence I created this book, which was designed not only to stand alone but also to be a companion to *Candlestick Charting Explained*. It serves as a study guide and boot-camp approach to learning. Its focus is on the salient and important points I made in the original book with an emphasis on a classroom environment complete with testing.

ACKNOWLEDGMENTS

I offer my sincere thanks and appreciation to Norman North for our 30 years of friendship and working together in the 1980s developing technical analysis software and, in particular, the CandlePower software that was the first commercially available software to identify Japanese candle patterns automatically. Wayne Corbitt needs special mention for all his effort in producing this book, along with numerous helpful suggestions and comments, he contributed greatly to Chapters 2 through 5. Wayne has written a book on candlesticks called, *All About Candlestick Charting*, that I highly recommend. Additionally, I have worked with Lynn Dufrenne and William Golson at Thomson Reuters over the years, along with many others at MetaStock, and I want to thank them sincerely for all their many contributions over the years. Lynn and William often have helped me refine an indicator concept. It helps to know people who are smarter than you. I always have to mention Steve Nison as the first to write about Japanese candlesticks. Steve coined many of the English names that we use. When I did my research, I decided it best not to change any of that. As in any publication signed by an author, any errors or omissions are clearly my responsibility.

1
ENLISTMENT: GETTING READY FOR DUTY

By purchasing this workbook, you have voluntarily enlisted to participate in doing battle with the markets. The markets are living, morphing entities that feed off of human emotion and trader losses. It is my intention to provide you with the weapons necessary to trade what you see, to help you harness the power of candlestick analysis, and to avoid unnecessary losses. We will start with the basics of candlestick lines and patterns and then add weapons to our arsenal as we progress. First, however, let me step you through my journey that has brought us together at this point in time.

WHY BOOT CAMP?

In 1971, after graduating from the University of Texas with a bachelor of science degree in aerospace engineering, I was faced with a country in recession, and the marketplace for new engineers was scarce, so I joined the United States Navy to become a fighter pilot. Of course, that meant that I had to become an officer, and that, in turn, meant that I had to attend Officer's Candidate School in Pensacola, Florida. No problem, right?

In October, 1971, I drove from Dallas, Texas, in my 1962 nonair-conditioned, faded-blue, four-door, standard transmission, six-cylinder Chevrolet Bel Air. This fine automobile had been with me since I was a junior in high school and had close to 175,000 miles. In the trunk, I had a box of my aerospace engineering books because I knew the Navy would be impressed and probably want me to teach others about aerodynamics, heat transfer, and boundary-layer theory. I started to include my golf clubs but later decided that I wouldn't have that much spare time between learning to be an officer, teaching aerodynamics, and engaging in all the social aspects of being a Navy pilot. Additionally, I had been a private pilot since 1967 and assumed that I knew all there was to know about flying airplanes. Wow, was I in for a shock!

After checking into a World War II barracks (I *knew* this was just temporary), I was told that I did not need anything from my car and would need only the clothes on my back. I was excited as I thought that I'd be issued my jet flight equipment and some officer uniforms. Then I was told to get a good night's rest and expect to get up fairly early. When I dropped off to sleep that night (the barracks was not air-conditioned), it was the last moment of that part of my life.

At 0500 hours (5 a.m., which later became 2 bells), I was startled awake with a horribly loud banging sound and someone yelling at me. The banging sound was made by a metal trash can being kicked down the hallway (which later became known as the passageway). The yelling came from a lean, muscular guy in a Marine drill instructor uniform, which was complete with a Smokey the Bear hat. Clearly, he was not aware of why I was there and had me confused with a felon, escaped convict, or something.

This was the beginning of a four-month period of my life that I honestly believe I can recall every single minute of because it was so dynamic, frightening, tiring, scary, disconcerting, exhausting—need I go on? If you have never been on the other side of a United States Marine drill instructor, you have missed one of life's remarkable events. His goal over the next four months was simple: break me down to almost nothing, and then build me up the way the Navy wanted me to be—an officer first, a pilot second. He did it.

I could write volumes on just those four months, but this isn't the place. Hence came the idea of calling this companion book to my *Candlestick Charting Explained* a "boot camp." It is designed to clarify, simplify, and quiz you on the details of Japanese candlestick analysis.

INTRODUCTION

I attended a Market Technician Association seminar in Phoenix, Arizona, in 1988. There was a large contingent of Japanese traders present, and they presented their charting techniques. It was the first time that I had ever heard of *Hi Ashi*, which is what the Japanese call their candlestick chart. I was working with N-Squared Computing then, and my colleagues and I decided to create a charting product using Japanese candle patterns with automatic recognition capability. I traveled to Japan and stayed with Takehiro Hikita, who was an active red bean and rice trader in Yokohama. I had known Hikita for years because he was a devoted customer of N-Squared Computing. He was intent on teaching me the art of candlestick analysis, as well as helping me to translate many of the books that are listed at the end of this book (see Sources).

There are many books out now on candle patterns, and most software programs have candlestick charting capability. However, very few have the correct (original Japanese) methodology. This book discusses *only* the candle patterns that came from original Japanese literature, with two exceptions: The Three Outside and Three Inside patterns were created when I was at N-Squared Computing to enhance the Engulfing and Harami patterns. They do this quite well, but please realize that they are *not* real Japanese candle patterns.

Note: I find it amusing that in new books on candlesticks, the Three Outside and Three Inside patterns generally are included as if they are actual Japanese candle patterns. I think only Steve Nison and I did any original research; the rest obtained their knowledge from us.

For additional study, I humbly recommend that you refer to the third edition of my book, *Candlestick Charting Explained*, published by McGraw-Hill. I cover all the patterns included in this book, the single-day patterns, and many others that were created to fill holes in the Japanese literature. This workbook closely follows the details laid out in that book, which was first published in 1992 and in its third edition includes a vast amount of statistics.

GENERAL COMMENTS AND OPINIONS

The following are "need to know" information pieces that I have put together in the last 20 years after giving numerous lectures and presentations on candlestick analysis. If you think that I have become opinionated over this time, you are correct. However, I always keep in mind that when dealing with an art form such as this, one should never speak in absolutes. Even though the following seems to be said absolutely, I am only expressing my opinion.

Why Are Single-Day Candle Patterns Not Recommended for Trading?

Every day the market sends a message. Here is what I say about single-day candlesticks: They are not candle patterns that allow you to see the evolution of trader psychology through multiple days, like you can with more complex candle patterns. I also say that single-day candlesticks still send a message that should neither be traded nor ignored.

Can You Use Candle Patterns on Intraday or Weekly Data?

Of course you can, but I don't recommend it. The Japanese were adamant about the period of time between the close of one day and the open of the next day as being critically important to the psychological evolution of traders in developing the pattern. With intraday charts, that time period is just the next data tick—not a lot of time to develop a thought. Weekly charts truly void the concept because the open is Monday's open, the close is Friday's close, the high is the high for the week (it could occur on any day of the week), and the low is the low for the week (again, it could occur on any day of the week). In fact, the open, high, and low all could occur on Monday, with the close on Friday. The trading activity for the last four days of the week would not be seen in a weekly candlestick. However, as with any art form, if it works for you, use it.

What Mistakes Do I See the Most in the Analysis of Candle Patterns?

Let's begin with a question: If you find a bullish reversal candle pattern, what does that mean? First, it is supposedly reversing something, right? What is it reversing? It is reversing the preceding trend. Second, if it is bullish reversal, wouldn't the preceding trend have to be down or bearish? Yes, and many people tend to ignore this critical element in pattern identification. Pattern analysis in isolation is poor analysis.

What Do You Use to Determine the Trend?

Originally, and in my book, I used a 10-period exponential average to determine the trend. If the midpoint of the body of the first day was above the 10-period average, then the trend was up. In an uptrend you can only have bearish reversal and bullish continuation patterns, and in a downtrend you can only have bullish reversal and bearish continuation patterns. Since that time, I have developed a proprietary method of trend analysis that is only available in my MetaStock add-on product, *Greg Morris' Japanese Candle Pattern Recognition*.

Price-based Support and Resistance

You will find that when candle patterns occur near support or resistance levels that are based on price, they generally will work better than when they are not. *Price-based* means that the support and resistance lines are horizontal. This works well because investors and traders all have a strong tendency to anchor on prices, whether from when they bought or when they sold.

Candle Pattern Filtering

I developed candle pattern filtering in the very early 1990s as an attempt to enhance the quality of signals generated from candle patterns. The concept is really quite simple. If you consider a common technical indicator such as Stochastics $\%D$, you know that whenever $\%D$ rises above 80, it is just a matter of time before it will drop back below 80 for a sell signal. I call this period of time when $\%D$ is above 80 the *bearish presignal area*. Thus, now if you also can find a bearish reversal candle pattern that occurs while $\%D$ is above 80, you are getting an emotionally driven sell signal *prior to* getting a technically based price sell signal. Of course, the inverse is to find bullish reversal patterns when $\%D$ is in its *bullish presignal area* below 20.

Think of the area above 80 and below 20 as the presignal area; it is a place where reversal patterns generally will fire before price-based indicators.

The Ideal Candle Pattern and Variations that Are Acceptable

There are many sketches of the candle patterns included in this book. Figure 1.1 shows you the "ideal" pattern. One rarely do you find the ideal pattern in real life and trading, but you must have some feel for what it should look like. You then can see how the pattern identi-

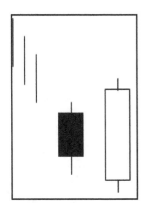

Figure 1.1 Engulfing+.

fied by a software program can vary from the ideal. In developing the software to identify candle patterns, I have kept the parameters fairly tight on the identification engine because the closer they are to ideal, the better they are generally. However, you cannot have the identification parameters too tight, or very few candle patterns would appear.

Why There Are More Reversal Patterns than Continuation Patterns

I think that it should be obvious that identifying the beginning and end of a trend is more important for trading than identifying that a trend is continuing. While the continuation patterns should not be ignored, they rarely offer a trading opportunity. They are more of a confirmation that the trend is still in place. However, if you did not take a position in the early stage of the trend, the continuation would be a second opportunity to place a trade.

Why There Are More Bullish Reversals than Bearish Reversals

If you have ever studied long-term charts of the markets or stocks, you can quickly see that when they are developing tops, they are usually long, drawn-out affairs (distribution), and the decision making of selling is more difficult for most investors. However, at bottoms, the emotions are quicker, and bottoms tend to be more sharp and defined. This is why there are more bullish reversal patterns than bearish reversal patterns.

2

THE FOUNDATION: PREPARING FOR BATTLE

Japanese candlestick analysis has been in existence for hundreds of years and is a valid form of technical analysis. Candlestick charting has its roots in the militaristic culture that was prevalent in Japan in the 1700s. One sees many terms throughout the Japanese literature on this topic that reference military analogies, such as the Three White Soldiers pattern presented in Chapter 3. Unlike more conventional charting methods, candlestick charting gives a deeper look into the mind-set of investors, helping to establish a clearer picture of supply/demand dynamics.

Japanese candlestick charts do not require anything new or different as far as price data are concerned. Open, high, low, and close are all that are needed to construct a candlestick chart. There are two main elements in the construction of a candlestick, the real body and the shadows.

The *real body* (Figure 2.1) is the box that makes up the difference between the opening and closing prices. The height of the body is the range between the day's opening price and the day's closing price. When the body is black, or filled, this means that the closing price was lower than the opening price on that day, which is considered

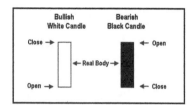

Figure 2.1. Candlestick real bodies.

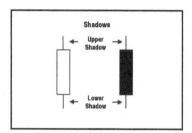

Figure 2.2. Candlestick shadows.

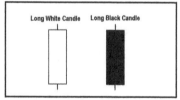

Figure 2.3. Long candles.

bearish. When the closing price is higher than the opening price, the body is white, or hollow, which is considered bullish.

Shadows (Figure 2.2) are the small, thin lines that can appear above and/or below the body. These lines represent the high and low prices reached during the trading day. The upper shadow represents the high price, and the lower shadow represents the low price. It is these shadows that give the appearance of a candle and its wick(s). Candles do not have to have shadows. In cases where the opening and closing prices also represent the high and low prices for the day, no shadow is present. These candles are called *Marubozu*, which are explained later in this chapter.

A *long day* or *long candle* (Figure 2.3) is a large price movement for the day between the opening and closing prices. In other words, the opening and closing prices are considerably different. Long days should be classified as such within the context in which they appear. It is best to use the most recent price action to determine what is long and what is not. Since Japanese candlestick analysis is based solely on short-term price movement, comparing the length of a candle with the most recent 5 to 10 candles should be adequate. Long white candles show dominance by buyers during the trading day, whereas long black candles show dominance by sellers.

Short days or *short candles* (Figure 2.4) also may be based on the same methodology as long days, with comparable results. There are also numerous days that do not fall into either the long or short day category. Short days represent indecision among traders because the opening and closing prices are very close. The color of the real body is not as important as the appearance of the short body itself. Short days are especially noteworthy when they appear in trending markets because they signify that a market that once was trending is now showing signs of a struggle for short-term price direction.

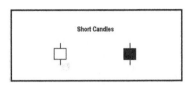

Figure 2.4. Short candles.

Marubozu means "close-cropped" or "close-cut" in Japanese. Other interpretations refer to it as a "bald or shaven head." In either case, the meaning reflects the fact that there is no shadow extending from the body at the open, the close, or both (Figure 2.5). Marubozu come in four types:

Black Marubozu. This is a long black body with no shadows at either end. This is considered an extremely weak line. It often becomes part of a bearish continuation or bullish reversal candle pattern, especially if it occurs during a downtrend.

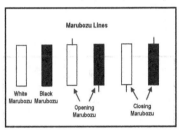

Figure 2.5. Marubozu lines.

White Marubozu. This is a long white body with no shadow on either end. This is an extremely strong line when considered on its own merits. Opposite of the Black Marubozu, it often is the first part of a bullish continuation or bearish reversal candle pattern.

Closing Marubozu. This has no shadow extending from the close end of the body, whether the body is white or black. If the body is white, there is no upper shadow because the close is at the top of the body. Likewise, if the body is black, there is no lower shadow because the close is at the bottom of the body. The Black Closing Marubozu is considered a weak line, and the White Closing Marubozu is considered a strong line.

Opening Marubozu. This has no shadow extending from the open price end of the body. If the body is white, there would be no lower

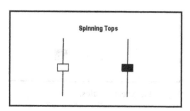

Figure 2.6. Spinning Tops.

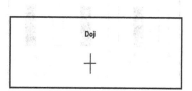

Figure 2.7. Doji.

shadow, making it a strong bullish line. The Black Opening Marubozu with no upper shadow is a weak and therefore bearish line.

Spinning Tops (Figure 2.6) are candlestick lines that have small real bodies with upper and lower shadows that are of greater length than the body's length. The color of the body of a Spinning Top, along with the actual size of the shadows, is not important. The small body relative to the shadows is what makes the Spinning Top. Spinning Tops carry much more weight because indecision patterns warn of a potential reversal when a market is trending. Their appearance in sideways or choppy markets has little meaning.

A *Doji* (Figure 2.7) occurs when the body of a candle line is so small that the open and closing prices are equal. The lengths of the shadows can vary. The perfect *Doji* has the same opening and closing prices, but some interpretation must be considered. If the difference between the opening and closing prices is within a few ticks (minimum trading increments), it is satisfactory.

Determining a *Doji* day is similar to the method used for identifying a long day; there are no rigid rules, only guidelines. If the previous days were mostly *Doji*, then the *Doji* day is not important. If the *Doji* occurs alone, this is a signal that there is indecision and must *not* be ignored. A *Doji* in a sideways, choppy market has little meaning, but a *Doji* in a trending market means that a trader needs to sit up and take notice. The appearance of a *Doji* does not guarantee a trend change; it merely warns that a trend change *could* occur. There are four specific types of *Doji* that each has its own implications for price behavior.

The *Long-Legged Doji* has upper and lower shadows in the middle of the day's trading range, clearly reflecting the indecision among buyers and sellers. Throughout the day, the market moved sharply higher and then sharply lower, or vice versa, before eventually closing at or near the opening price. Figure 2.8 shows an example of a Long-Legged *Doji*.

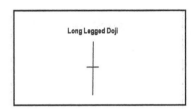

Figure 2.8. Long-Legged Doji.

The *Gravestone Doji* (Figure 2.9) develops when the *Doji* is at or very near the low of the day. If the upper shadow is quite long, this means that the Gravestone *Doji* is much more bearish. Prices open and trade higher all day only to close where they opened, which is also the low for the day. This cannot possibly be interpreted as anything but a failure to rally.

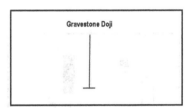

Figure 2.9. Gravestone Doji.

The *Dragonfly Doji* (Figure 2.10) occurs when the open and close are at the high of the day. The appearance of a Dragonfly *Doji* at the end of a downtrend is extremely bullish. In this case, a Dragonfly *Doji* shows that sellers were able to drive the price lower during the day but were unable to sustain downward price movement because price closed at the same level that it opened, which is also the high of the day.

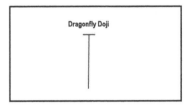

Figure 2.10. Dragonfly Doji.

The *Four-Price Doji* is very rare and occurs when all four price components are equal, or the open, high, low, and close are all the same price. This line could occur when a stock is very illiquid or when the data source did not have any prices other than the close. Futures traders should not confuse this with a limit move. It is so rare that one should suspect data errors. However, it does represent complete and total uncertainty by traders in market direction. Figure 2.11 shows an example of a Four-Price *Doji*.

Figure 2.11. Four-Price Doji.

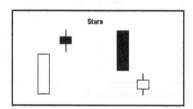

Figure 2.12. Stars.

A *Star* (Figure 2.12) appears whenever a small body gaps above or below the previous day's long body. Ideally, the gap should encompass the shadows, but this is not always necessary. A star indicates uncertainty in the marketplace. Stars are part of many candle patterns, but typically reversal patterns.

QUESTIONS

1. The price-data elements necessary to construct a candlestick chart are the
   A. open and close.
   B. high and low.
   C. midpoint of the day's range and the close.
   D. open, high, low, and close

2. The real body of the candle is the difference between
   A. the high and low prices for the day.
   B. the opening and closing prices for the day.
   C. the low and closing prices for the day.
   D. the high and opening prices for the day.

3. Which of the following is a *true* statement about shadows?
   A. They appear above and below the real body.
   B. They represent the highest and/or lowest prices for the day.
   C. Candles do not always have shadows.
   D. All the above.

4. Which of the following is *true* of long candles?

   A. They are considered long relative to the size of the 5 to 10 previous candles.

   B. A long white candle shows indecision among traders.

   C. A long black candle shows dominance by buyers.

   D. All the above.

5. Which of the following is *true* of short candles?

   A. Their color is very meaningful.

   B. They have the most meaning in trending markets.

   C. They show indecision among traders.

   D. Both B and C.

6. Which of the following is *true* of *Marubozu*?

   A. A Black *Marubozu* is a considered a strong line.

   B. A Closing *Marubozu* has no shadow at the close end of the candle.

   C. An Opening *Marubozu* has a shadow at the open end of the candle.

   D. A White *Marubozu* can have a shadow at either end.

7. A characteristic of a Spinning Top is

   A. a short real body.

   B. that the color of the real body is not important.

   C. that it has shadows that typically are longer than the real body length.

   D. all the above.

8. Which of the following is *true* of a *Doji*?

    A. It shows indecision among traders.

    B. Its opening and closing prices are virtually equal.

    C. It is of little meaning in a trending market.

    D. Both A and B.

9. Which of the following is *not* a valid *Doji* classification?

    A. Shaven-Head *Doji*

    B. Gravestone *Doji*

    C. Dragonfly *Doji*

    D. Long-Legged *Doji*

10. Examine the chart below and identify the type of candle line that is circled.

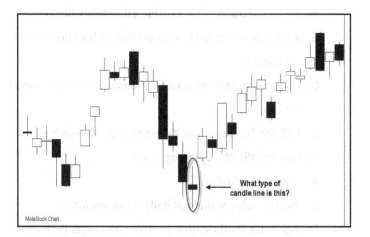

A. Black *Marubozu*

B. Gravestone *Doji*

C. Spinning Top

D. Long candle

3

REVERSAL PATTERNS: REPELLING THE ADVANCE

Reversal patterns alert a trader that a shift in market psychology may be occurring and that a change in price direction may be near. Think of reversal patterns as an attacking army (buyers or sellers) being repelled and sounding a retreat, allowing the other side to begin a push in the opposite direction. These patterns or warnings can occur in as little as one day or in some cases as many as five days. Owing to the short-term predictive nature of candlesticks, their implications are usually short term, but this does not mean that they can't signal the early stages of longer-term trading opportunities. The key to understanding and using reversal patterns effectively is being able to identify them and then exercising the patience to wait for price confirmation that a reversal indeed has occurred. This chapter is divided into sections for one-day patterns, two-day patterns, three-day patterns, and four-day or more patterns. This is a rather long chapter because there are many patterns to cover, but take your time and become familiar with these patterns and the psychology behind them.

As each pattern is introduced, a reference will be given to its discussion in the book *Candlestick Charting Explained* (or *CCE*) along with the appropriate page numbers. For example, if something is on pages 20 and 21 in the book, it will appear as (*CCE* 20–21). Referencing the book will provide a deeper understanding of these patterns. *Candlestick Charting Explained* also contains other less frequently occurring reversal patterns that will not be discussed here.

When identifying and using reversal patterns, it is important to note that in order for them to be worthy of consideration, the market *must* be trending either higher or lower. After all, if they are called *reversal patterns*, they need something to reverse. Their appearance in choppy or sideways markets greatly diminishes their importance. Also, always make note of prior highs and lows to use as potential support and resistance levels. A bullish reversal pattern that occurs at prior support has a greater chance of success. The same goes for bearish reversal patterns at prior resistance.

ONE-DAY PATTERNS

A *Hammer* or *Hanging Man* (*CCE* 27–31) is a pattern that has the same appearance, but its label and meaning is derived from the context in which it appears. These patterns have small real bodies and longer lower shadows that are at least twice the length of the real body. Figure 3.1 shows an example of these patterns.

The Hammer forms in a downtrending market and is so named because the market is trying to "hammer out a bottom." Its appearance shows that price opened at or near its high and then sold off sharply during the day. Buyers then emerged to push the closing price back near the open, leaving a long lower shadow. The failure

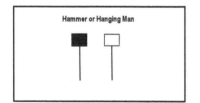

Figure 3.1. Hammer and Hanging Man.

of the market to continue the selloff reduces the bearish sentiment, and most traders will be uneasy with any bearish positions they might have. While a Hammer is labeled as such regardless of the real body color, a white body is slightly more bullish because it shows that buyers were able to push the closing price back above the opening price. These patterns ideally should not have any upper shadow, but a vey small upper shadow is permissible. The daily chart of Conoco Phillips (COP; Figure 3.2) shows an example of a Hammer.

Figure 3.2. Hammer–Conoco Phillips daily. (MetaStock.)

A Hanging Man occurs at the top of a trend or during an uptrend. Its name comes from the fact that this candle looks somewhat like a man hanging. For the Hanging Man, the market is considered bullish because of the uptrend. In order for the Hanging Man to appear, the price action for the day must trade much lower than where it opened and then rally to close near the high. This causes long lower shadows, which show that the market just might begin a selloff. If the market opens lower the next day, those holding long positions may look for an opportunity to sell, thus forcing prices lower. Again, in this case, the color of the real body is not important for identification purposes, but a black real body is slightly more bearish because it shows that sellers were able to keep the price below the opening

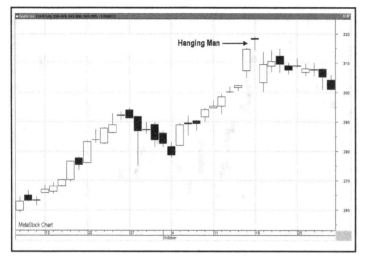

Figure 3.3. Hanging Man–Apple, Inc., daily.
(METASTOCK.)

price, showing net distribution during the session. The daily chart of Apple, Inc. (AAPL; Figure 3.3), shows an example of a Hanging Man.

A *Belt Hold line* (CCE 33–35) is also classified as an Opening *Marubozu* because there is no shadow from the opening end of the candlestick. The bullish Belt Hold is a white Opening *Marubozu* that occurs in a downtrend. It opens on the low of the day, rallies significantly against the trend, and then closes at or near the high. The bearish Belt Hold is a black Opening *Marubozu* that occurs in an uptrend. Similarly, it opens on the high, trades against the trend of the market, and then closes at or near its low. Figure 3.4 shows examples of Belt Hold lines.

A Belt Hold occurs when the market is trending and a significant gap occurs in the direction of the trend on the open. From that point, the market never looks back. All further price action that day is in the opposite direction of the previous trend. This causes much concern, and many positions will be covered or sold, which will help to accentuate the reversal. The daily chart of CB Richard Ellis Group, Inc. (CBG; Figure 3.5), shows an example of a bullish Belt Hold, which in this case also happens to be a Piercing Line, discussed later in this chapter.

The daily chart of Starbucks Corp. (SBUX; Figure 3.6) shows an example of a bearish Belt Hold. Notice how price opened at its high

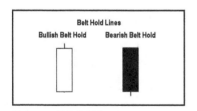

Figure 3.4. Belt Hold lines.

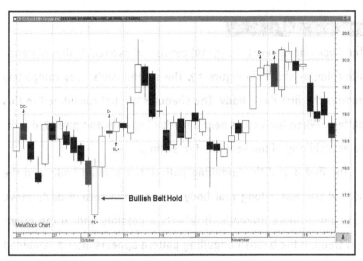

Figure 3.5 Bullish Belt Hold—CB Richard Ellis Group, Inc., daily.
(METASTOCK WITH JCPR ADD-ON.)

for the day and then moved decisively lower throughout the session. This particular Belt Hold also was a bearish Engulfing pattern, which is discussed later in this chapter.

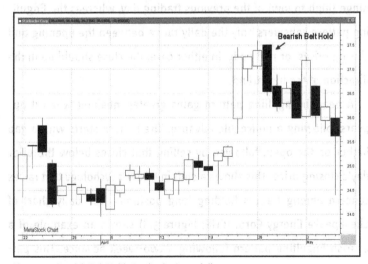

Figure 3.6 Bearish Belt Hold—Starbucks Corp. daily.
(METASTOCK.)

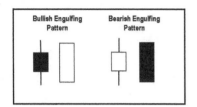

Figure 3.7. Engulfing patterns.

TWO-DAY LINES

The *Engulfing pattern* (*CCE* 35–39) consists of two real bodies of opposite color, as shown in Figure 3.7. The second day's body completely engulfs the first day's body. The shadows are not considered in this pattern. When this occurs near a market top or in an uptrend, it indicates a shifting of the sentiment to selling.

The first day of the Engulfing pattern has a small body, and the second day has a long real body. Because the second day's move is so much more dramatic, it reflects a possible end to the previous trend. If the bearish Engulfing pattern appears after a sustained move, it increases the chance that most bulls are already long. In this case, there may not be enough new money (bulls) to keep the market uptrend intact.

An Engulfing pattern is similar to the traditional outside day with one difference. The outside day needs to trade outside the entire range (high to low) of the previous trading day, whereas the Engulfing pattern considers only the daily range between the opening and closing prices, or real body. In either case, the close should be in the direction of the new trend.

A bearish Engulfing pattern gains greater meaning when it appears following a noticeable advance. The pattern starts with a gap higher on the open, followed by selling that closes below the prior day's closing price. This shows a shift in trader psychology that raises concern among traders holding long positions. The daily chart of Chesapeake Energy Corp. (CHK; Figure 3.8) shows an example of a bearish Engulfing pattern following a two-week advance. This pat-

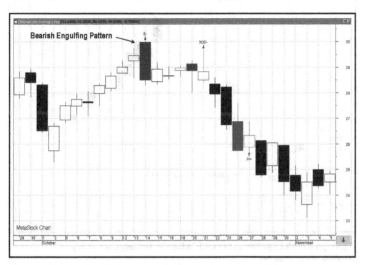

Figure 3.8 Bearish Engulfing pattern—Chesapeake Energy Corp. daily.
(METASTOCK WITH JCPR ADD-ON.)

tern was a signal that sentiment was turning against CHK, and a three-week decline followed.

A bullish Engulfing pattern forms when sentiment changes from negative to positive on a stock. The day starts with a gap lower from the previous day's close before reversing and closing above the prior day's close. This provides a warning to those holding short positions that market sentiment may be changing. Any upside movement the following day may be exacerbated by the closing out of positions by nervous shorts. The daily chart of CF Industries Holdings, Inc. (CF; Figure 3.9) shows the formation of a bullish Engulfing pattern after a multiday decline. A 2½-week rally followed.

The *Harami pattern* (CCE 40–45) is made up of the opposite arrangement of days as the Engulfing Pattern. *Harami* is the Japanese

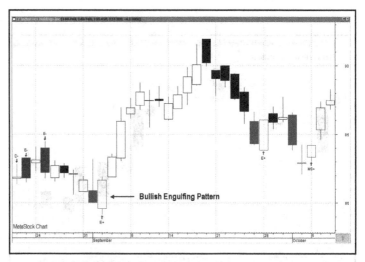

Figure 3.9 Bullish Engulfing pattern—CF Industries Holdings, Inc., daily.
(METASTOCK WITH JCPR ADD-ON.)

word for "pregnant" or "body within." In most instances, the *Harami* patterns are opposite in color, also like the Engulfing pattern. The *Harami* is quite similar to the traditional inside day, but like the Engulfing Pattern, only the real bodies are considered for pattern identification. Shadows are ignored. The *Harami* requires that the body of the second day be completely engulfed by the first day. Figure 3.10 shows examples of *Harami* patterns.

A bullish *Harami* pattern occurs after the market has been in a downtrend for some time. A long black day with average volume has occurred which helps perpetuate the bearishness. The next day, prices open higher which shocks any complacent bears, causing the price to rise further. The price rise is tempered by the usual late comers seeing this as an opportunity to short the trend they missed the first time. Volume on the second day should exceed the first day,

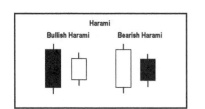

Figure 3.10. Harami patterns.

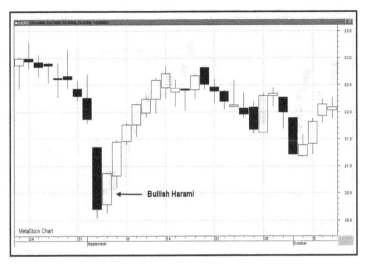

Figure 3.11. Bullish Harami–CA, Inc., daily.
(METASTOCK.)

which shows strong short covering. The daily chart of CA, Inc. (CA; Figure 3.11), shows an example of a bullish Harami. Notice how the real body of the white candle is completely inside the black candle from the previous day. A higher close on the third day would provide the needed proof that the trend has reversed.

A bearish *Harami* is formed when an uptrend is in place and is perpetuated with a long white day and high volume. The next day prices open lower and stay in a small range throughout the day, closing even lower but still within the previous day's body. In view of the sudden deterioration of trend, traders should become concerned about the strength of this market, especially if volume is light. It certainly appears that the trend is about to change. Confirmation on the third day would be a lower close. The daily chart of Apartment Investment & Management Company (Figure 3.12) shows an example of

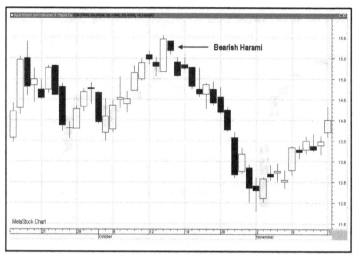

Figure 3.12. Bearish Harami—Apartment Investment & Management Company daily. (METASTOCK.)

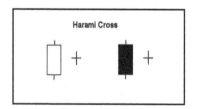

Figure 3.13. Harami cross.

a bearish *Harami*. Notice the sharply lower close on the day following formation of the *Harami*, which confirmed a reversal lower.

A *Harami Cross* pattern (*CCE 45–49*) consists of a long body followed by a smaller body. It is the relative size of these two bodies that make the *Harami* Cross important. Remember that *Doji* days, where the open and close price are equal, represent days of indecision. Therefore, small-body days that occur after long-body days also can represent a day of indecision. The more indecision and uncertainty, the more likelihood there is of a trend change. Figure 3.13 shows an example of a *Harami* Cross.

The *Harami* Cross is a rare but powerful pattern. When it occurs after a prolonged trend, it shows great indecision among traders and warns of a pending reversal. This is a two-level pattern in that it combines the reversal characteristics of the *Harami* with the *Doji*. The

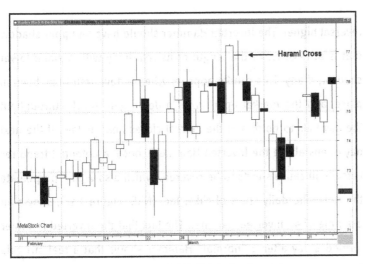

Figure 3.14. Bearish Harami Cross—Stanley Black & Decker, Inc., daily. (METASTOCK.)

daily chart of Stanley Black & Decker, Inc. (SWK; Figure 3.14), shows an example of a bearish *Harami* Cross because the day of indecision followed a long white candle in an uptrend. The bullish *Harami* Cross would be the opposite. The day of indecision would follow a long black candle in a downtrend.

The *Inverted Hammer* and *Shooting Star* patterns (*CCE* 49–54) are essentially the same candle line as far as construction goes, but they each convey a different meaning. Their name and implications are derived from the context in which they appear. Figure 3.15 shows examples of these lines.

The Inverted Hammer is a bottom reversal line. Similar to its cousin, the Hammer, it occurs in a downtrend and represents a possible reversal of trend. Common to most single and double candlestick patterns, it is important to wait for bullish verification to confirm a

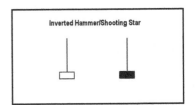

Figure 3.15. Inverted Hammer and Shooting Star.

reversal higher. The Inverted Hammer should have an upper shadow that is at least twice the length of its real body with a small lower shadow, if any. This candle appears when a downtrend has been in place, and the market opens with a down gap. A rally throughout the day fails to hold, and the market closes near its low. If the next day opens above the Inverted Hammer's body, a potential trend reversal will cause shorts to be covered, which also would perpetuate the rally. The daily chart of Nike, Inc. (NKE; Figure 3.16), shows an example of an Inverted Hammer. The fact that the Inverted Hammer formed a day after a "normal" Hammer shows that a real struggle for control of price direction was developing. Notice the confirmation of a reversal the very next day as price moved higher and closed well above the real body of the Inverted Hammer.

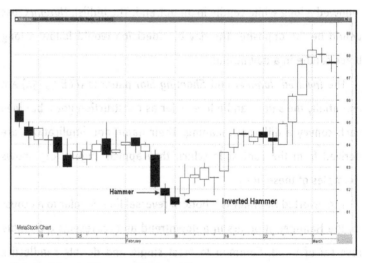

Figure 3.16. Inverted Hammer—Nike, Inc., daily.
(METASTOCK.)

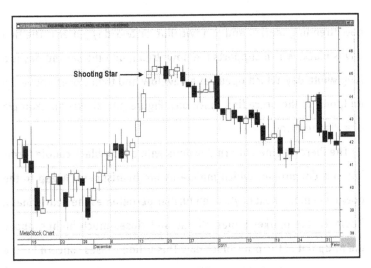

Figure 3.17. Shooting Star–NII Holdings, Inc., daily.
(METASTOCK.)

The Shooting Star is a single-line pattern that indicates an end
to an upward move. It is not a major reversal signal. A rally attempt
was completely aborted when the close occurred near the low of
the day. The body of the Shooting Star does in fact gap above the
previous day's body, which makes this also a two-candle reversal
pattern because the real body of the previous day's candle also must
be considered. The appearance of this pattern after a gap higher during an uptrend would give bulls a good reason to bank profits, thus
fueling any developing reversal. The body color of the shooting star
is not as important as the appearance of the candle line itself, but a
black body would be considered slightly more bearish than a white
body. The daily chart of NII Holdings, Inc. (NIHD; Figure 3.17), shows
an example of a Shooting Star.

The *Piercing Line* (CCE 55–58) is a bullish pattern that occurs in a

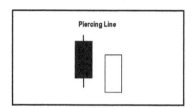

Figure 3.18. Piercing Line.

downtrending market and is a two-line or two-day pattern. The first day is black, which supports the downtrend, and the second day is a long white day, which opens at a new low and then closes above the midpoint of the preceding black day. Figure 3.18 shows an example of a Piercing Line.

The Piercing Line pattern develops with a long black candle forming in a downtrend, which maintains the bearishness. A gap to the downside in the next day's open further perpetuates the bearishness. However, the market rallies all day and closes much higher, above the midpoint of the prior black day. This action causes concern for the bears, and a potential bottom has been made.

The daily chart of Republic Services, Inc. (RSG; Figure 3.19), shows an example of a Piercing Line forming at support in March

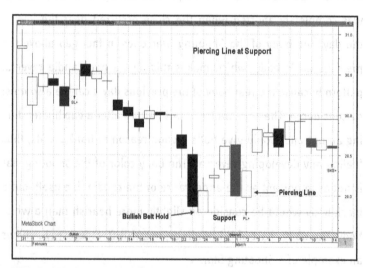

Figure 3.19 Piercing Line—Republic Services, Inc., daily.
(METASTOCK WITH JCPR ADD-ON.)

2011. The Piercing Line found support right at the low of the Bullish Belt Hold that formed just a few days before. This increased the odds of an upside bounce in price. Always make use of prior highs and lows to help determine the likelihood of reversal patterns succeeding.

The *Dark Cloud Cover* (CCE 58–61) is the bearish counterpart to the Piercing Line. Because this pattern occurs in an uptrend, the first day is a long white day. The second day gaps above the high of the white candle before reversing lower and closing below the midpoint of the white candle. It is important to note that the second day's open must be above the upper shadow if one exists, not just above the high of the white candle's real body. Figure 3.20 shows an example of a Dark Cloud Cover.

The Dark Cloud Cover develops when a long white candle is formed in an uptrend, adding to bullish sentiment. The next day, the market gaps over the high of the white candle and then trades lower the rest of the day, closing below the midpoint of the white candle. Traders who were bullish now will be forced to rethink their positions. Their liquidation of positions contributes to the reversal. The daily chart of Norfolk Southern Company (NSC; Figure 3.21) shows an example of the Dark Cloud Cover. Price had advanced throughout the month of December 2010 before forming the Dark Cloud Cover on January 11, 2011. Price then formed four straight *Harami* within the real body of the Dark Cloud Cover, showing trader uncertainty. Once price broke below the low of the real body of the Dark Cloud Cover (the *dashed line*), a signal was given that the

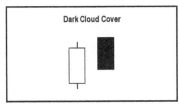

Figure 3.20 Dark Cloud Cover.

Figure 3.21 Dark Cloud Cover—Norfolk Southern Company daily.
(METASTOCK WITH JCPR ADD-ON.)

reversal was underway. NSC then declined more that 7 percent over the next seven days.

The *Doji Star* (CCE 63–65) provides a warning that the trend is about to change. This two-candle pattern starts with a long real body (black in a downtrend or white in an uptrend). The second day starts with a gap opening in the direction of the trend, with the open and close virtually equal, forming a *Doji*. A bearish reversal in an uptrend is referred to as an *Evening Star*, whereas a bullish reversal in a downtrend is referred to as a *Morning Star*. Figure 3.22 shows examples of *Doji* Stars.

In either case, the psychology of the market turns abruptly from one of going with the trend to one of doubt because the opening gap in the direction of the trend could not be sustained. The appearance of the *Doji* is one of uncertainty as buyers and sellers

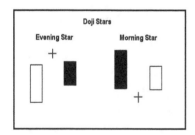

Figure 3.22 Doji Stars.

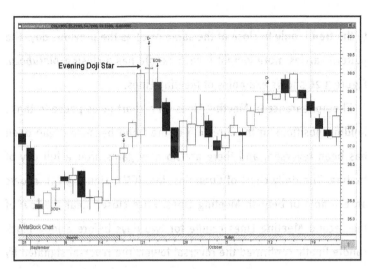

Figure 3.23 Evening Doji Star–Genuine Parts Company daily.
(METASTOCK WITH JCPR ADD-ON.)

struggle for control of the market–hardly a sign of a healthy trend. The daily chart of Genuine Parts Company (GPC; Figure 3.23) shows an example of an Evening *Doji* Star pattern. If you look very closely, you will notice the slight space between the opening and closing prices of the *Doji* candle, but this is considered close enough because the difference between the opening and closing prices was 0.03. Following the *Doji* Star, a long black candle formed, confirming the reversal lower.

Meeting Lines (CCE 66–70) are formed when opposite-colored candles have the same closing price. Meeting Lines are also referred to as *Counterattack Lines*. This is a two-candle pattern that consists of a long line in the direction of the trend, followed by a candle on the second day (preferably a long candle) that gaps in the direction of the trend at the open and then spends the rest of the day moving counter

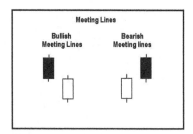

Figure 3.24. Meeting Lines.

to the trend, only to close at the same price as the previous day. The pattern carries more weight if each candle has a closing *Marubozu*. Figure 3.24 shows examples of Meeting Lines.

The appearance of Meeting Lines on a chart gives pause to those holding positions in the direction of the trend because a gap open has been reversed, and there are no new gains after a full day of trading. The daily chart of Cummins, Inc. (CMI; Figure 3.25), shows an example of bearish Meeting Lines. Price closed near the low of the second Meeting Lines candle for two days before a long black candle finally confirmed the reversal lower. The reversal signaled by this pattern caused Cummins to drop over 16 percent over the next two weeks.

The *Homing Pigeon* (*CCE* 70–72) closely resembles the *Harami* pat-

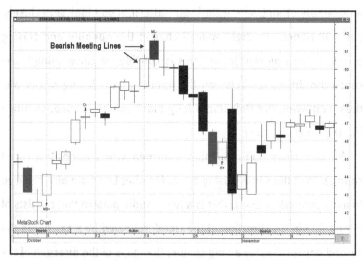

Figure 3.25. Bearish Meeting Lines—Cummins, Inc., daily.
(METASTOCK WITH JCPR ADD-ON.)

tern, except that both bodies are black rather than opposite in color. Figure 3.26 shows an example of a Homing Pigeon pattern.

The Homing Pigeon forms when the market is in a downtrend, evidenced by a long black day. The next day, price opens higher, trades completely within the previous day's body, and then closes slightly lower. Depending on the previous trend, this shows a reduction in selling pressure and raises expectations of a price reversal higher. The daily chart of Chevron Corp. (CVX; Figure 3.27) shows an example of a Homing Pigeon reversal.

The *Matching Low* consists of two black candles that have the same low price on consecutive days. It starts with a long black candle in a downtrend, followed by a higher open the next day. The second day's action is negative following the open, however, and price closes at

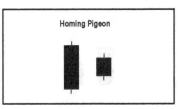

Figure 3.26. Homing Pigeon.

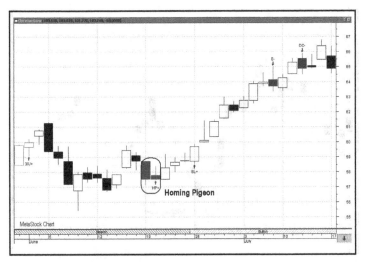

Figure 3.27. Homing Pigeon—Chevron Corp. daily.
(METASTOCK WITH JCPR ADD-ON.)

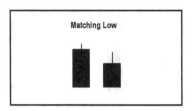

Figure 3.28. Matching Low.

the previous day's low. The fact that price closed poorly but did not violate the previous day's closing price shows short-term support and increases the likelihood of a price reversal higher. Figure 3.28 shows an example of a Matching Low pattern.

The daily chart of Alcoa, Inc. (AA; Figure 3.29), shows an example of a Matching Low. Notice how the second candle in the Matching Low had a small real body and looked to be a cross between a Spinning Top and a Hammer. This was a second piece of evidence that a reversal higher in price was likely.

The *Kicking pattern* (*CCE* 83–87) is formed when a gap occurs between two *Marubozu* candles of opposite colors. A bullish Kicking pattern occurs when a Black *Marubozu* is followed by a White *Marubozu*, whereas a bearish Kicking pattern is formed by a White

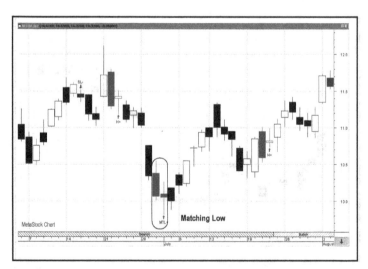

Figure 3.29. Matching Low–Alcoa, Inc., daily.
(METASTOCK WITH JCPR ADD-ON.)

Marubozu followed by a Black *Marubozu*. Unlike other reversal patterns, the direction of the market is not as much of a consideration with the Kicking pattern. Figure 3.30 shows examples of Kicking patterns.

The strength of the Kicking pattern is evidenced by the gap in the opposite direction following a strong bullish or bearish day. There is some flexibility with the pattern. Even though the textbook version consists of two straight *Marubozu*, small shadows are permissible. The main thing to look for is a long candle followed by a gap in the other direction by a long candle of the opposite color. This abrupt change in psychology shows that further price movement in the direction of the Kicking pattern is likely. The daily chart of The Home Depot (HD; Figure 3.31) shows an example of a bearish Kicking pat-

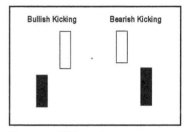

Figure 3.30. Kicking pattern.

Figure 3.31. Bearish Kicking—The Home Depot, Inc., daily.
(METASTOCK WITH JCPR ADD-ON.)

tern. An ideal Kicking pattern does not have any shadows, but that is quite restrictive, so minimal shadows in both number and length are acceptable.

THREE-DAY PATTERNS

The *Morning Star* and *Evening Star* (*CCE* 94–98) are three-day reversal patterns that have serious reversal implications when they appear in a trending market. The Morning Star is a bullish reversal pattern. Its name indicates that it foresees higher prices. It is made of a long black body followed by a small body that gaps lower. The color of the middle (or star) candle is not important. The third day is a white body that moves into the first day's black body. An ideal Morning Star would have a gap before and after the middle (star) day's body. Figure 3.32 shows an example of a Morning Star.

The *Evening Star* is the bearish counterpart to the Morning Star. Because the Evening Star is a bearish pattern, it appears after or during an uptrend. The first day is a long white body followed by a star. Remember that a star's body gaps away from the previous day's body and that its color is not important. The star's smaller body is the first sign of indecision. The third day gaps down and closes even lower, completing this pattern. Figure 3.33 shows an example of an Evening Star.

The daily chart of Apartment Investment & Management Company (AIV; Figure 3.34) shows an example of a Morning Star. The main point to consider is that the middle or star candle has a small body

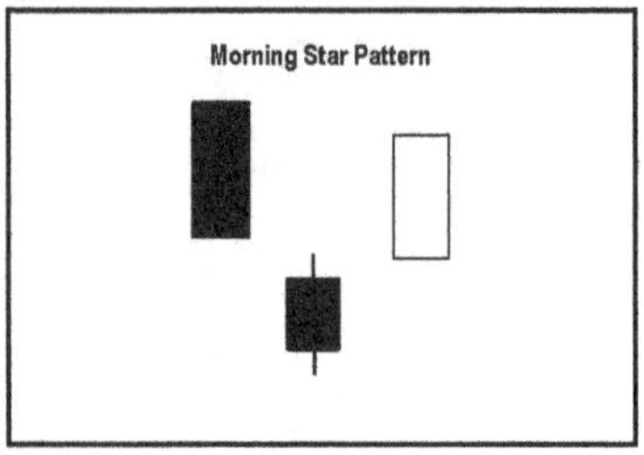

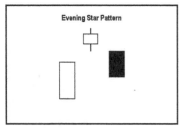

Figure 3.32. Morning Star.

Figure 3.33. Evening Star.

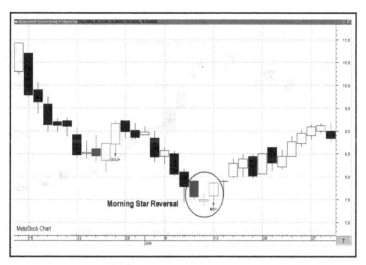

Figure 3.34. Morning Star reversal–Apartment Investment & Management Company.
(METASTOCK WITH JCPR ADD-ON.)

that gaps away from the previous day's low and then gaps higher on the third day. In this example, the star candle is actually a Spinning Top, which by itself is a warning of a possible change in sentiment and trend.

The daily chart of NVIDIA Corp. (NVDA; Figure 3.35) shows an example of an Evening Star reversal. Notice that the first candle of the pattern is a long white candle, which reinforces the trend. The second candle has a small body that gaps away from the long white candle. The third candle is a black candle that gaps down and away from the star candle before closing into the body of the first day's white candle. Price then proceeded to drop over 20 percent in three weeks.

The *Morning Doji Star* and *Evening Doji Star* (CCE 99–103) have even stronger reversal implications than the regular Morning Star or Evening Star reversals because the middle or star candle is a

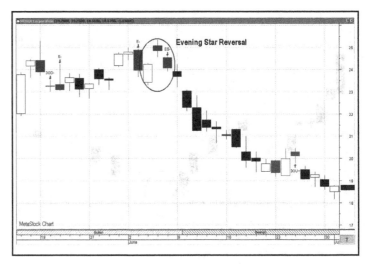

Figure 3.35. Evening Star reversal–NVIDIA Corp. daily.
(METASTOCK WITH JCPR ADD-ON.)

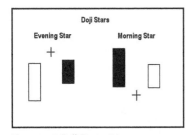

Figure 3.36. Doji Star patterns.

Doji. Figure 3.36 shows examples of the Morning and Evening Doji Star reversals.

The Morning *Doji* Star forms in a downtrend when a long black candlestick is followed by a *Doji* Star. Just like the regular Morning Star, confirmation on the third day fully supports the reversal of trend. This type of Morning Star, the Morning *Doji* Star, can represent a significant reversal. It is therefore considered more significant than the regular Morning Star pattern. The daily chart of Sears Holding Corp. (SHLD; Figure 3.37) shows an example of a Morning *Doji* Star reversal.

The Evening *Doji* Star forms in an uptrend as a long white candle is followed by a *Doji* Star. The next day, price gaps lower and forms a black candle that closes into the body of the first day's white candle. The regular Evening Star has a small real body as its star, whereas the Evening *Doji* Star has a *Doji* as its star. The Evening *Doji* Star is more

Figure 3.37. Morning Doji Star reversal—Sears Holding Corp. daily.
(METASTOCK WITH JCPR ADD-ON.)

important because of this *Doji*. The daily chart of News Corp. (NWSA; Figure 3.38) shows an example of an Evening *Doji* Star reversal.

Remember, the psychology behind the *Doji* Star reversal is similar

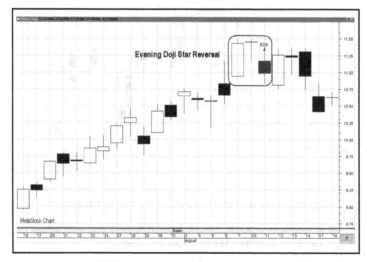

Figure 3.38. Evening Doji Star reversal—News Corp. daily.
(METASTOCK WITH JCPR ADD-ON.)

to that of the regular Morning and Evening Star patterns, except that the *Doji* Star is more of a shock to the previous trend and therefore more significant.

The *Abandoned Baby* (CCE 103–107) is almost exactly the same as the Morning and Evening Doji Star patterns with one important exception. Here, the shadows of the *Doji* also must gap below the shadows of the first and third days for the Abandoned Baby bottom, whereas the opposite is true for the Abandoned Baby top. The Abandoned Baby is quite rare. The daily chart of The Home Depot, Inc. (HD; Figure 3.39), shows an example of an Abandoned Baby top. The middle candle of the pattern also formed a Deliberation pattern, which is discussed later in this chapter.

Figure 3.39. Abandoned Baby top–The Home Depot, Inc., daily.
(METASTOCK WITH JCPR ADD-ON.)

The *Upside Gap Two Crows* pattern (*CCE* 111–114) occurs only in up-trends. As with most bearish patterns, it begins with a white-body candlestick. The gap referred to in the name of this pattern is the gap between not only the first and second days but also the first and third days. The second and third days are black, which is where the two crows originate. The third day (second black day) should open higher and then close lower than the close of the second day. The third day, even though gapping and closing lower than the second day, still is gapped above the first day. Simply said, the second black day engulfs the first black day. Figure 3.40 shows an example of the pattern.

Like the beginning of most bearish reversal patterns, a white-body day occurs in an uptrend. The next day opens with a higher gap, fails to rally, and closes lower, forming a black day. This is not too wor-

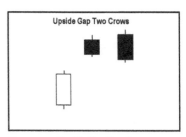

Figure 3.40. Upside Gap Two Crows.

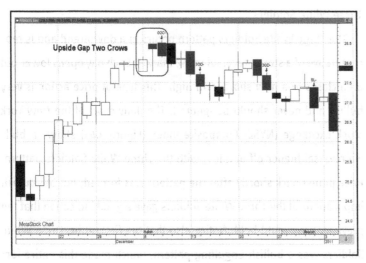

Figure 3.41. Upside Gap Two Crows—ABAXIS, Inc., daily.
(METASTOCK WITH JCPR ADD-ON.)

risome because it still did not gap lower than the first day's close. On the third day, prices gap again to a higher open and then drop to close lower than the previous day's close. The closing price, however, is still above the close of the white first day. The bullishness is bound to subside. How can you have two successively lower closes and still be a raging bull? The daily chart of ABAXIS, Inc. (ABAX; Figure 3.41), shows an example of the Upside Gap Two Crows pattern. Notice that the discussion of the gaps and daily closes relates only to the real bodies of the candles, not the shadows.

The *Three White Soldiers* pattern (CCE 125–128) shows a series of long white candlesticks that close at progressively higher prices. It is also best if prices open in the middle of the previous day's range (body). This stair-step action is quite bullish and shows that the downtrend has ended abruptly. Figure 3.42 shows an example of Three White Soldiers.

The Three White Soldiers pattern occurs in a downtrend and is representative of a strong reversal in the market. Each day opens lower but then closes to a new short-term high. This type of price action is very bullish and never should be ignored. The daily chart of the New York Stock Exchange (NYSE) Composite Index (Figure 3.43) shows a bullish reversal higher off of a low with the Three White Soldiers pattern. Price pulled back shortly after the pattern was formed, but the bullish implications of the Three White Soldiers gave a good indication that the previous low would hold. Notice also that the first of the Three White Soldiers was a bullish Engulfing pattern, which made this entire formation an even stronger signal that price was about to reverse higher.

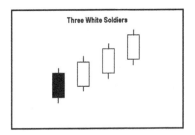

Figure 3.42. Three White Soldiers.

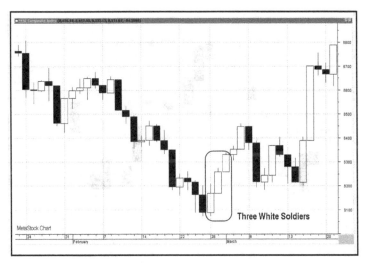

Figure 3.43. Three White Soldiers—NYSE Composite Index daily.
(METASTOCK.)

Three Black Crows (CCE 128–131) is the counterpart of the Three White Soldiers pattern. Occurring during an uptrend, three long black days are stair-stepping downward. Each day opens slightly higher than the previous day's close but then drops to a new closing low. When this occurs three times, a clear message of trend reversal has been sent. Figure 3.44 shows an example of Three Black Crows.

The Three Black Crows pattern forms when the market is either approaching a top or has been at a high level for some time. A decisive trend move to the downside is made with a long black day. The next two days are accompanied by further erosion in prices caused by much selling and profit-taking. This type of price action has to take its toll on the bullish mentality. The daily chart of NetApp, Inc. (NTAP; Figure 3.45), shows an example of Three Black Crows.

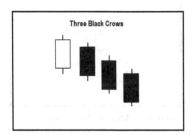

Figure 3.44. Three Black Crows.

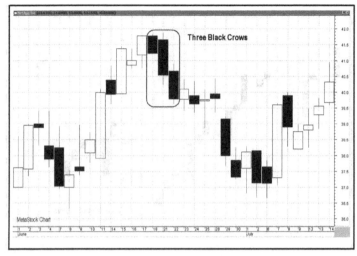

Figure 3.45. Three Black Crows—NetApp, Inc., daily.
(METASTOCK.)

The *Advance Block* pattern (*CCE* 135–138) is a derivation of the Three White Soldiers pattern. However, it must occur in an uptrend, whereas the Three White Soldiers must occur in a downtrend. Unlike the Three White Soldiers pattern, the second and third days of the Advance Block pattern show weakness. The long upper shadows show that the price extremes reached during the day cannot hold. This type of action after an uptrend and then for two days in a row should make any bullish market participants nervous, especially if an uptrend is getting overextended. Figure 3.46 shows an example of the Advance Block pattern.

The scenario of the Advance Block pattern closely resembles the events that could take place with the Three White Soldiers pattern. This situation, however, does not materialize into a strong advance.

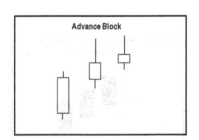

Figure 3.46. Advance Block pattern.

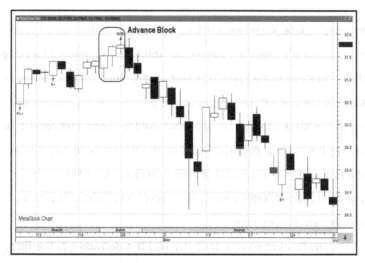

Figure 3.47. Advance Block—Paychex, Inc., daily.
(METASTOCK WITH JCPR ADD-ON.)

Rather, it weakens after the first day because the close is significantly lower than the high. The third day is as weak as the second day. Remember, weakness in this context is relative to the Three White Soldiers pattern. The daily chart of Paychex, Inc. (PAYX; Figure 3.47), shows an example of the Advance Block pattern.

The *Descent Block* pattern (*CCE* 138–141) is a three-day bullish reversal pattern. This pattern was not a part of the original Japanese literature and was created as a complement to the Advance Block pattern. The Descent Block pattern shows a weakening of the downtrend that gives bearish traders pause and leads to a price reversal higher. Figure 3.48 shows an example of a Descent Block pattern.

The first day of the pattern is a long black day in an established downtrend. The second day is also a black day that closes below the

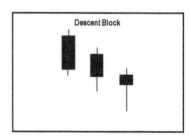

Figure 3.48. Descent Block pattern.

first day's close. After two black days, the current downtrend seems secure, and the bears are happy. The third day is another black day that closes below the low of the second day, which makes the bears become complacent. The key, however, is that each day the real bodies of the black candles are shrinking, which shows less conviction during the trading day. The fact that the third candle has a lower shadow says that a reversal of some sort may have already begun. The daily chart of Netflix, Inc. (NFLX; Figure 3.49), shows an example of a Descent Block pattern.

The *Deliberation* pattern (*CCE* 143–147) is a derivative of the Three White Soldiers pattern. The main difference is that the Deliberation pattern occurs at the end of an existing trend, not the beginning of a new trend like Three White Soldiers. The smaller real body on the

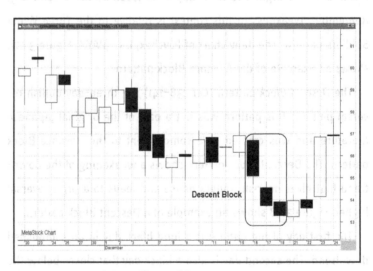

Figure 3.49. Descent Block—Netflix, Inc., daily.
(METASTOCK.)

third candle of this pattern shows indecision on the part of traders, which signals that a change in price direction may be near. Figure 3.50 shows examples of the Deliberation pattern.

The *Bearish Deliberation* pattern is a three-day reversal pattern. The pattern begins with two consecutive long white days that make new highs in an uptrend. It is best if the third day gaps above the second day. The third, small-bodied candle shows the indecision necessary to arrest the up move. This indecision is the time of deliberation. A further confirmation easily could turn this pattern into an Evening Star. This pattern exhibits weakness similar to the Advance Block pattern in that it gets weak in a short period of time. The difference is that the weakness occurs all at once on the third day. The daily chart of E. I. du Pont Nemours and Company (DD; Figure 3.51) shows an

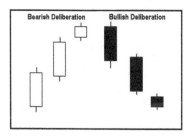

Figure 3.50. Deliberation pattern.

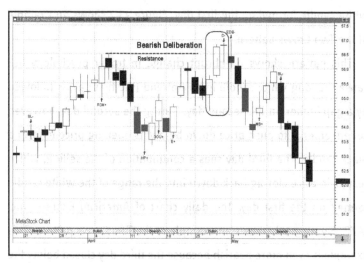

Figure 3.51. Bearish Deliberation pattern—E. I. du Pont Nemours and Company daily.
(METASTOCK WITH JCPR ADD-ON.)

example of a Bearish Deliberation pattern. Notice how price gapped lower after the Deliberation pattern that formed an Evening *Doji* Star. The fact that this pattern also occurred in the 56.50 area that formed resistance in early April increased the odds of success for this reversal pattern.

The *Bullish Deliberation* pattern was not a part of the original Japanese literature and was created as a reciprocal to the Bearish Deliberation pattern. The concept is the same, except that this pattern culminates with an abrupt end to a downtrend.

The *Two Crows* pattern (*CCE* 148–151) is good only as a topping reversal or bearish pattern. It typically appears at the end of an extended up move and consists of a long white day followed by a black candle that gaps higher before closing poorly. The third day of the pattern consists of a black candle that closes well into the body of the white candle formed on the first day. Figure 3.52 shows an example of the Two Crows pattern.

This pattern shows an abrupt change in trader psychology because the long white candle in an uptrend (the first day) is followed by a gap higher on the second day. During the second day, however, sellers emerge to push price down below its opening price to form a black candle. The third day sees a continuation of the selling, which results in price closing back down into the range of the white candle formed on the first day. The daily chart of American Express, Inc. (AXP; Figure 3.53), shows an example of the Two Crows pattern. This example is even more bearish because the third day closed below the low of the first day, showing that sellers were firmly in control.

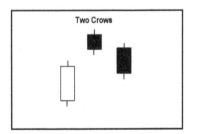

Figure 3.52. Two Crows pattern.

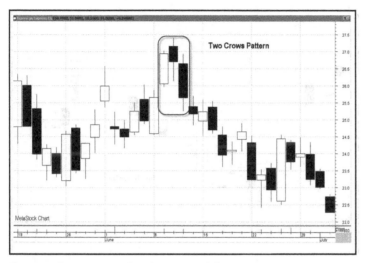

Figure 3.53. Two Crows–American Express, Inc., daily.
(METASTOCK.)

The *Three Inside Up* and *Three Inside Down* patterns (*CCE* 155–158) are confirmations for the *Harami* pattern. The first two days are exactly the same as a *Harami*, with the third day as a confirming close day with respect to the bullish or bearish case. These patterns are not found in any Japanese literature. We developed them to assist in improving the overall results of the *Harami* pattern, and they have done quite well. Figure 3.54 shows examples of the Three Inside Up and Three Inside Down patterns.

The Three Inside Up pattern is formed when a bullish *Harami* is followed by a third day that closes higher, above the high of the first candle. The close of the third candle confirms the reversal that was indicated by the formation of the *Harami* pattern and shows the resolve of buyers to take price higher. The daily chart of Dominion Resources, Inc. (D; Figure 3.55), shows an example of a Three Inside Up

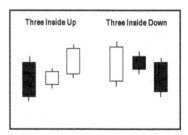

Figure 3.54. Three Inside Up and Three Inside Down patterns.

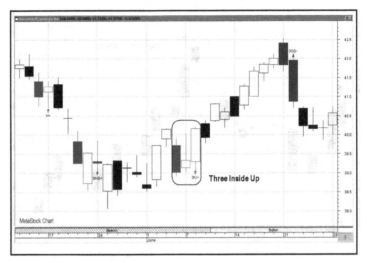

Figure 3.55. Three Inside Up–Dominion Resources, Inc., daily.
(METASTOCK WITH JCPR ADD-ON.)

pattern. Notice that the first two days of the pattern are merely an unresolved *Harami* pattern, whereas adding the third day provides solid confirmation that the bulls are in control.

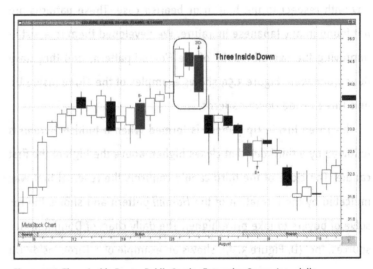

Figure 3.56. Three Inside Down–Public Service Enterprise Group, Inc., daily.
(METASTOCK WITH JCPR ADD-ON.)

The Three Inside Down pattern shows the tide turning from bull-ishness to bearishness in an uptrend. The daily chart of Public Service Enterprise Group, Inc. (PEG; Figure 3.56), shows the *Harami* formed during the uptrend, followed by confirmation of a reversal lower. This showed that one day of consolidation or indecision (the *Harami*) was followed by sellers stepping up and forcing price lower.

The *Three Outside Up* and *Three Outside Down* patterns (*CCE* 159–162) are confirmation for Engulfing patterns. The concept is identical to Three Inside Up and Three Inside Down and how they work with the *Harami*. Here, the Engulfing pattern is followed by either a higher or lower close on the third day depending on whether the pattern is up or down. The Three Outside Up and Three Outside Down patterns are not found in Japanese literature. We developed them to assist in improving the overall results of the Engulfing pattern, and they have done quite well. Figure 3.57 shows examples of the Three Outside Up and Three Outside Down patterns.

The first part of the Three Outside Up pattern is a two-day bullish Engulfing pattern. This pattern in and of itself is a bullish sign, but it is foolish to trade on a pattern before price confirms the implica-tions of the pattern. In other words, wait for bullish price activity to confirm the bullish reversal pattern. The third day of the Three Day Up pattern provides that confirmation because price closes higher than the engulfing day. The daily chart of AMR Corp. (AMR; Figure 3.58) shows an example of a Three Day Up pattern. Notice the strong advance that followed.

Just as the Three Day Up pattern provides reversal confirmation

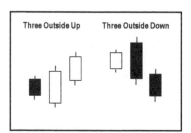

Figure 3-57. Three Outside Up and Three Outside Down patterns.

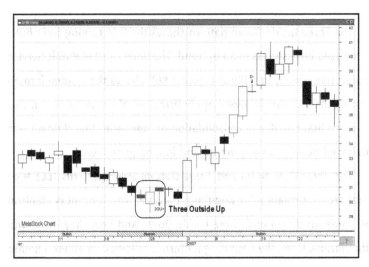

Figure 3.58. Three Outside Up–AMR Corp. daily.
(METASTOCK WITH JCPR ADD-ON.)

for a bullish Engulfing pattern, the Three Day Down pattern contains
confirmation for the bearish Engulfing pattern. The daily chart of Con-
Way, Inc. (CNW; Figure 3.59), shows an example of the Three Outside

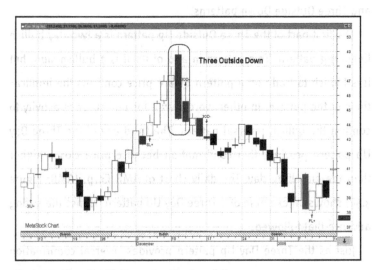

Figure 3.59. Three Outside Down–Con-Way, Inc., daily.
(METASTOCK WITH JCPR ADD-ON.)

Down pattern. The bearish Engulfing pattern shown on the second day of the pattern is very strong, as demonstrated by its size. The third day provided confirmation that a move lower was underway.

Note: The Three Inside Up, Three Inside Down, Three Outside Up, and Three Outside Down patterns were created to enhance the statistical performance of the *Harami* and Engulfing patterns. Merely adding a third day with a closing price in the direction of the pattern vastly improved them. They are *not* original Japanese candle patterns and do not appear in any Japanese literature, even though you may find them in other candlestick books.

The *Three Stars in the South* pattern (CCE 163–165) shows a deteriorating downtrend with less and less price movement and consecutively higher lows. The long lower shadow on the first day is crucial to this pattern because it shows signs of buying enthusiasm, as shown by the lower shadow. The next day opens higher, trades lower, but does not go lower than the previous day's low. The second day also closes off its low. The third day is a Black *Marubozu* and is engulfed by the previous day's range. Figure 3.60 shows an example of Three Stars in the South.

The daily chart of NVR, Inc. (NVR; Figure 3.61), shows an example of the Three Stars in the South pattern. Notice the long black candle on the first day with a noticeable lower shadow that demonstrates buying interest. The second day is within the range of the first day, whereas the third day is within the range of the second day. This lack of follow-through selling is a signal that price is likely to reverse higher. The third candle is not a *Marubozu*, but its real body and its

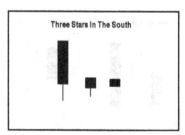

Figure 3.60. Three Stars in the South.

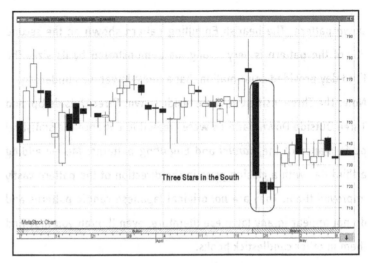

Figure 3.61. Three Stars in the South—NVR, Inc., daily. (METASTOCK.)

entire daily range are inside the second day's candle, which shows continuing indecision for sellers.

The *Stick Sandwich* (*CCE* 169–175) is a pattern that consists of two like-colored candles "sandwiched" around a candle of the opposite color. The two like-colored candles must have the same closing price. The same closing price either forms support for a bullish Stick Sandwich or resistance for a bearish Stick Sandwich. This support or resistance increases the odds of a price reversal. Figure 3.62 shows examples of the Stick Sandwich.

The bullish Stick Sandwich consists of two black bodies that have a white body between them. The closing price of the two black candles must be equal. A support price has been found, and the opportunity for price to reverse higher is quite good.

The bearish Stick Sandwich is a three-day bearish reversal pattern

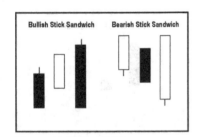

Figure 3.62. Stick sandwich.

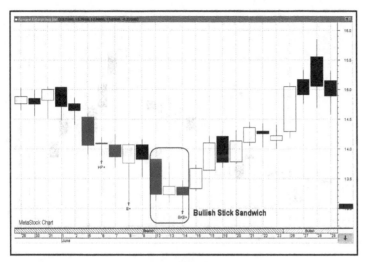

Figure 3.63. Bullish Stick Sandwich–Apogee Enterprises, Inc., daily.
(MetaStock with JCPR add-on.)

that was created as the complement to the bullish Stick Sandwich pattern. It consists of two white bodies that have a black body between them. The matching closing prices of the two white candles forms resistance, which means that a price reversal lower is quite possible. The daily chart of Apogee Enterprises, Inc. (APOG; Figure 3.63), shows an example of a bullish Stick Sandwich.

Identical Three Crows (CCE 133–134) is a bearish reversal pattern that is a close relative of the Three Black Crows. The difference is that in the Identical Three Crows pattern, days two and three open at or near the previous day's close. Figure 3.64 shows an example of Identical Three Crows.

This pattern resembles panic selling and should cause additional downside action. Each day's close sets a benchmark for opening prices on the next trading day. There is a total absence of buying

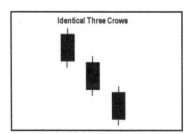

Figure 3.64. Identical Three Crows.

Figure 3.65. Identical Three Crows—Caterpillar, Inc., daily. (METASTOCK.)

power with this pattern. The daily chart of Caterpillar, Inc. (CAT; Figure 3.65), shows an example of the Identical Three Crows pattern. Notice the small gap open between days one and two, which added more evidence of market weakness at that time.

FOUR-DAY OR MORE PATTERNS

The *Breakaway* pattern (*CCE* 181–185) is a bullish five-day pattern that occurs during a downtrend and represents an acceleration of selling to a possible oversold position. The pattern starts with a black day followed by another black day whose body gaps down. After the down gap, the next three days set consecutively lower prices. All days in this pattern are black, with the exception of the third day, which may be either black or white. The three days after the gap are similar

to the Three Black Crows in that their highs and lows are each consecutively lower. The last day completely erases the small black days
and closes inside the gap between the first and second days. The
bearish Breakaway pattern is not discussed in the Japanese literature. I decided to test such a pattern as the reciprocal to the bullish
Breakaway pattern, and I discovered that it works quite well. Figure
3.66 shows examples of the Breakaway pattern.

It is important to realize what is being accomplished here: The
trend has accelerated with a big gap and then starts to fizzle, but it
still moves in the same direction. The slow deterioration of the trend is
quite evident from this pattern. Finally, a burst in the opposite direction completely recovers the previous three days' price action. What
causes the reversal implication is that the gap has not been filled. A

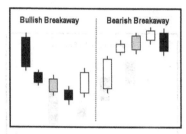

Figure 3.66. Breakaway.

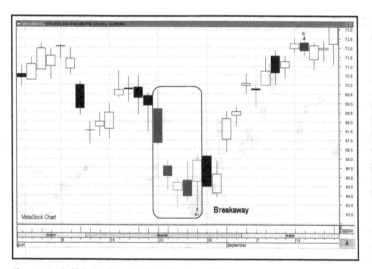

Figure 3.67. Bullish Breakaway—Caterpillar, Inc., daily.
(METASTOCK WITH JCPR ADD-ON.)

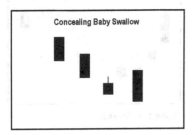

Figure 3.68. Concealing Baby Swallow.

short-term reversal has taken place. The daily chart of Caterpillar, Inc. (CAT; Figure 3.67), shows an example of a bullish Breakaway pattern.

The *Concealing Baby Swallow* pattern (*CCE* 186–189) is a four-day bullish reversal pattern that starts with two Black *Marubozu* days that support the downtrend. On the third day, the downtrend begins to deteriorate with a period of trading above the opening price. This is especially important because the open was gapped down from the previous day's close. The fourth day completely engulfs the third day, including the upper shadow. Even though the close is at a new low, the velocity of the previous downtrend has eroded significantly, and shorts should be protected. Figure 3.68 shows an example of the Concealing Baby Swallow pattern.

Although the four straight black days in a downtrend generally are

Figure 3.69. Concealing Baby Swallow–E. I. du Pont de Nemours Company daily.
(MetaStock.)

considered bearish, the pause and brief show of strength on the third day should be enough to give pause to even the most ardent bears. The daily chart of E. I. du Pont de Nemours and Company (DD; Figure 3.69) shows an example of the Concealing Baby Swallow pattern.

A *Ladder Bottom* (*CCE* 189–192) is a downtrend with four consecutive lower closes and black days. The fourth of these black candles trades higher than the open, which produces an upper shadow, but ultimately closes at a new low for the decline. The upper shadow on the fourth day is the first indication of buying interest, even though price closed at a new low. The fifth day closes much higher than the previous day or two. Figure 3.70 shows an example of a Ladder Bottom.

This pattern develops during a period of complacency for the bears. After a good move to the downside, prices trade above the open price

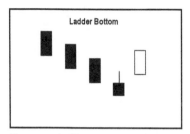

Figure 3.70. Ladder Bottom.

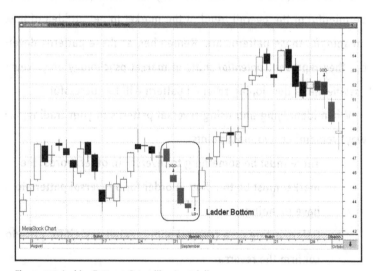

Figure 3.71. Ladder Bottom–Caterpillar, Inc., daily.
(METASTOCK WITH JCPR ADD-ON.)

and almost reach the high price of the previous day, but then they close at another new low. This action certainly will get the attention of the shorts and shows that the market will not go down forever. The shorts will rethink their position, and if profits are good, the next day they will sell. Their action causes a gap up on the last day of the pattern, and the close is considerably higher. If volume is high on the last day, a trend reversal probably has occurred. The daily chart of Caterpillar, Inc. (CAT; Figure 3.71), shows an example of a Ladder Bottom.

SUMMARY

When attempting to master these patterns, it is best to start with the simpler one- and two-day patterns and work your way up to the more complex three- and four-day and more patterns. Always be mindful of the overall trend of the market to get an idea of how meaningful these patterns are. Remember, as these patterns develop, they represent *potential* shifts in market psychology only. Never *assume* that a developing reversal pattern will be successful.

When identifying and using reversal patterns in your trading, always remember two main points:

1.   There must be something to reverse—in other words, the market must be trending in order for a reversal pattern to have meaning.

2.   Before acting on a reversal pattern, always wait for price to confirm the reversal.

Another consideration when evaluating the quality of a reversal pattern is whether it is forming at a former support or resistance area. When these areas come into play, such as a bullish reversal pattern at support or a bearish reversal pattern at resistance, the odds for a successful reversal are enhanced.

An exercise I highly recommend is to take some time and go through as many charts as you can to try to identify trends and any reversal patterns that appear. Have this chapter handy so that you can understand the psychology behind each pattern as these reversals unfold. This will help you to properly identify reversal patterns that have a higher probability of success.

QUESTIONS

1. Reversal patterns are most important when they occur
   A. over a three- or four-day period.
   B. in a sideways or choppy market.
   C. in a trending market.
   D. All the above

2. Which of the following is *not true* of a Hammer?
   A. A Hammer is a warning signal of a possible reversal in an uptrend.
   B. A Hammer ideally should not have an upper shadow, but a small shadow is permissible.
   C. A Hammer should have a lower shadow at least twice the length of its real body.
   D. The appearance of a Hammer is a warning signal to bearish traders.

3. Belt Hold lines
   A. occur in both uptrends and downtrends.
   B. form an opening *Marubozu*.
   C. gap in the direction of the trend at the open before reversing.
   D. All the above

4. Which of the following is *not* a one-day reversal pattern?
   A. Hammer
   B. Engulfing pattern
   C. Belt Hold
   D. Hanging Man

5. Which of the following is *true* of an Engulfing pattern?
   A. It is similar to the traditional inside day.
   B. The second candle needs to engulf only the real body of the previous candle.
   C. It can occur only in uptrends.
   D. The second candle needs to engulf the entire previous candle, including the shadows.

6. Which of the following is *true* of the *Harami* pattern?
   A. The entire second candle (shadows and all) must be contained within the previous candle.
   B. The second candle engulfs the first candle.
   C. Only the real bodies are considered in the *Harami* pattern.
   D. Both A and B.

7. Which of the following is *true* of a *Harami* Cross?

   A. It is a rare pattern.

   B. The second candle forms a *Doji*.

   C. The indecision and uncertainty of the pattern increase the likelihood of a trend change.

   D. All the above

8. Which of the following is *true* of a Shooting Star?

   A. A Shooting Star indicates the end of an upward move.

   B. A Shooting Star is a major reversal signal.

   C. A Shooting Star begins the day with a gap higher in price.

   D. Both A and C.

9. Which of these statements is *not true* of the Piercing Line pattern?

   A. A Piercing Line occurs in a downtrend.

   B. The second candle must gap lower in the direction of the trend at the open.

   C. The second candle only needs to open below the real body of the first candle.

   D. The second candle must close above the midpoint of the first candle.

10. Which of these statements best describes the Dark Cloud Cover?

   A. A Dark Cloud Cover forms in an uptrend.

   B. The second candle gaps higher in the direction of the trend at the open.

C. The second candle must close below the midpoint of the first candle.

D. All the above

11. Which of the following statements is *true* regarding the *Doji* Star?

A. It is a common pattern.

B. It is a one-day pattern.

C. It comes in two types, Evening and Morning Star.

D. It shows strong conviction among traders.

12. Which of the following statements is *true* of Meeting Lines?

A. They are formed when closing prices match on consecutive opposite-colored candles.

B. Their appearance gives pause to those holding positions in the direction of the trend.

C. The pattern carries more weight if each candle has a Closing *Marubozu*.

D. All the above

13. Which of the following patterns is a bullish reversal pattern that consists of a small-bodied candle with gaps between the candles before and after it?

A. Morning Star

B. Evening Star

C. Spinning Top

D. *Harami*

14. Which bearish three-day reversal pattern contains a *Doji* on the second day that must gap above the shadows of the first and third days?
    A. Three Black Crows
    B. Three White Soldiers
    C. Abandoned Baby Top
    D. Upside Gap Two Crows

15. Which of the following are characteristics of the Three White Soldiers pattern?
    A. Each day opens lower but then closes at a new short-term high.
    B. Its appearance means that an uptrend is ready to end.
    C. The stair-step action shows that the downtrend has ended abruptly.
    D. Both A and C.

16. Which of the following are characteristics of the Three Black Crows pattern?
    A. It occurs when a downtrend has been in effect for some time.
    B. Each day opens slightly higher than the previous day's close but then drops to a new closing low.
    C. It is a sign of hope for the bulls.
    D. Both A and C.

17. Which pattern is a derivative of the Three White Soldiers pattern but shows developing weakness in an uptrend?

    A. Three White Knights

    B. Advance Block

    C. Evening *Doji* Star

    D. Descent Block

18. Which of the following are characteristics of the Two Crows pattern?

    A. The first day is a long white candle, followed by a gap higher and a poor close on the second day.

    B. It is a bearish reversal pattern.

    C. The black candle on the third day must close well into the body of the first day's white candle.

    D. All the above

19. Which pattern provides reversal confirmation for the *Harami* pattern?

    A. Three Outside Down or Three Outside Up

    B. Three Inside Down or Three Inside Up

    C. Three Stars in the South

    D. Stick Sandwich

20. Which pattern provides reversal confirmation for the Engulfing pattern?

    A. Three Outside Down or Three Outside Up

    B. Three Inside Down or Three Inside Up

    C. Three Stars in the South

    D. Stick Sandwich

21. Which pattern shows a deteriorating downtrend with less and less price movement and consecutively higher lows?

    A. Identical Three Crows

    B. Three White Soldiers

    C. Three Stars in the South

    D. Three Dark Elves

22. Which of the following best describes the Stick Sandwich pattern?

    A. It consists of two like-colored candles "sandwiched" around a candle of the opposite color.

    B. The two like-colored candles must not have the same closing price.

    C. A bullish Stick Sandwich has two black bodies with a white body between them.

    D. Both A and C.

23. Which of the following is *true* of the Identical Three Crows pattern?

    A. It resembles panic selling and should cause additional downside action.

    B. It is a sign of hope for the bulls.

    C. There is a total absence of buying power with this pattern.

    D. Both A and C.

24. Which of the following patterns is *not* a valid four-day or more pattern?

   A. Breakaway

   B. Concealing Baby Swallow

   C. Five-Day Sumo Split

   D. Ladder Bottom

25. Which of the following are important points to remember when trading off of reversal patterns?

   A. Reversal patterns should be traded as soon as they begin to develop to get a jump on other traders.

   B. Prior support and/or resistance areas can give greater weight to reversal patterns.

   C. Always wait for price to confirm reversals before trading them.

   D. Both B and C.

26. What is the name of the reversal pattern shown in the chart below?

   A. Bearish Engulfing pattern

   B. Dark Cloud Cover

   C. Bearish Crow pattern

   D. Evening Star

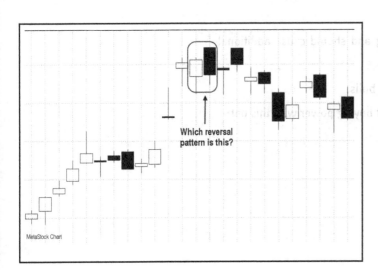

Which reversal pattern is this?

MetaStock Chart

27. What is the name of the reversal pattern shown in the chart
   to the right?
   A. Bearish Stick Sandwich
   B. Bearish Engulfing pat-
      tern
   C. Dark Cloud Cover
   D. Meeting Lines

28. What is the name of the
   reversal pattern shown in
   the chart below?
   A. Bullish Engulfing pattern
   B. Bullish Stick Sandwich
   C. Concealing Baby Swallow
   D. Homing Pigeon

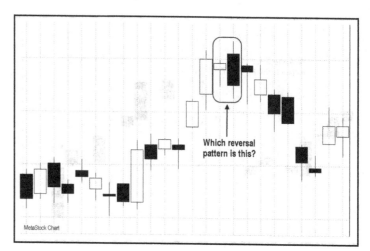

Which reversal pattern is this?

MetaStock Chart

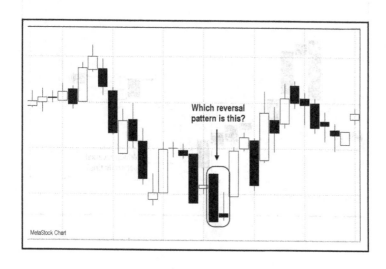

Which reversal pattern is this?

MetaStock Chart

29. What is the name of the reversal pattern in the chart to the left?

A. Belt Hold

B. Evening Star

C. Morning Star

D. Dark Cloud Cover

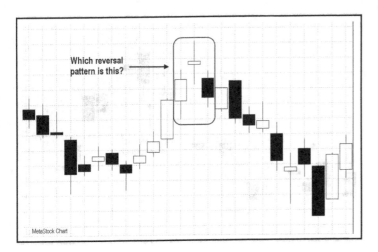

30. What is the name of the reversal pattern in the chart below?

A. Morning Star

B. Ladder Bottom

C. Bullish Engulfing pattern

D. Piercing Line

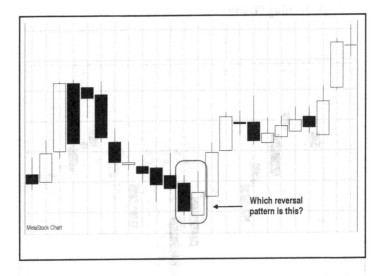

4

CONTINUATION PATTERNS: THE NEXT ATTACK WAVE

A *continuation pattern* represents a period of rest for price action during the prevailing trend. In militaristic terms, think of this time as an army resting before it launches its next offensive (trend continuation). Unlike reversal patterns, which warn of a pending change in price direction, continuation patterns offer a chance to either establish new positions or add to existing positions in the direction the market is already moving. While no trade entry is risk-free, the odds are better stacked in favor of the trader when he or she trades in the direction of existing capital flows. Just as with reversal patterns, a trend must be in place for these patterns to have meaning. Since these are labeled *continuation patterns*, there must be a *trend* in place to *continue*. In many cases, these patterns occur at the end of price consolidations during larger-degree trends where price has been rather directionless for a period of time, which gives the appearance of a period of rest as stated earlier. This chapter is organized in the same fashion as Chapter 3 of *Candlestick Charting Explained*. The continuation patterns discussed will be split into two-day, three-day, and four-day or more patterns and also will contain page references to the book, *Candlestick Charting Explained* (CCE).

TWO-DAY PATTERNS

Separating Lines (CCE 213–217) have the same open and are opposite in color. They are similar to but the opposite of Meeting Lines. The second day of these patterns is a Belt Hold candlestick. The bullish pattern has a white bullish Belt Hold, and the bearish pattern has a black bearish Belt Hold. Separating Lines should be two long lines, but there is no requirement that this be so. In other words, an element of flexibility is allowed for identification of this pattern. Figure 4.1 shows examples of bullish and bearish Separating Lines.

Separating Lines reinforce the existing trend following a day of doubt. In an uptrend, a black day occurs that casts doubt on the strength of the uptrend. The following day, price gaps higher and opens at the previous day's open. Price moves sharply higher from there, forming a long white candle that once again establishes that

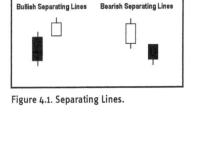

Figure 4.1. Separating Lines.

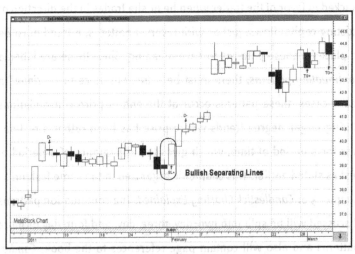

Figure 4.2 Bullish Separating Lines—The Walt Disney Company daily.
(METASTOCK WITH JCPR ADD-ON.)

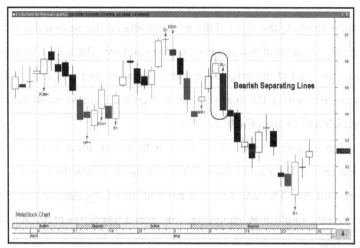

Figure 4.3 Bearish Separating Lines—E. I. du Pont de Nemours and Company daily.
(METASTOCK WITH JCPR ADD-ON.)

buyers are in control. The daily chart of The Walt Disney Company (DIS; Figure 4.2) shows an example of bullish Separating Lines. Notice how the formation of the Separating Lines pattern signals the end of the sideways consolidation period.

In a downtrend, a white candle forms that is followed by a black candle that gaps lower and opens at the same price as the previous day's white candle. The price action continues lower and forms a long black candle, showing that sellers are firmly in control. The daily chart of E. I. du Pont de Nemours and Company (DD; Figure 4.3) shows an example of bearish Separating Lines.

The bearish version of the *On-Neck Line* pattern (*CCE* 217–223) is actually an undeveloped Piercing Line with the second day's close occurring at the low of the previous day. This means that if there is a

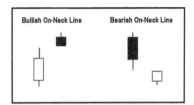

Figure 4.4. On-Neck Line.

lower shadow, the close of the white candle on the second day is at the lowest point of that shadow, not the real body. The bullish version was not part of the original Japanese literature and was created as a complement to the bearish pattern. Figure 4.4 shows examples of bullish and bearish On-Neck Lines.

The bearish On-Neck Line starts with a long black candle in a downtrend. The second day is white and opens below the low of the previous day. This day does not need to be a long day, or it might resemble a bullish Meeting Line. The second day closes at the low of the first day.

The bearish On-Neck Line usually appears during a decline. Bear-ishness is increased with the long black first day. The market gaps down on the second day but cannot continue the downtrend. As the market rallies, it is stopped at the previous day's low price. This must be uncomfortable for the bottom fishers who go into the market that

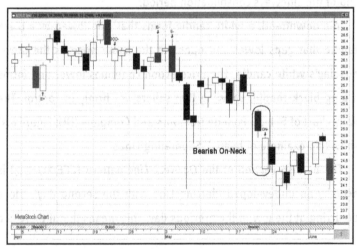

Figure 4.5 Bearish On-Neck Line—AT&T, Inc., daily.
(METASTOCK WITH JCPR ADD-ON.)

day. The downtrend should continue shortly. The daily chart of AT&T, Inc. (T; Figure 4.5), shows an example of a bearish On-Neck Line.

The *In-Neck Line* (*CCE* 223–229) is similar to the On-Neck Line pattern, with the In-Neck Line closing near the *close* of the previous day. The bearish In-Neck Line is another version of a failed bullish Piercing Line. Just as with the On-Neck Line pattern, the bullish version of the In-Neck Line was not part of the original Japanese literature and was created as a complement to the bearish In-Neck Line. Figure 4.6 shows examples of the In-Neck Line.

The bearish In-Neck Line begins with a black candle in a downtrend. The second day is a white day with an opening price below the first day's low. The close of the second day is just barely into the real body of the first day. For all practical purposes, the closes are equal.

The psychology behind the bearish In-Neck Line is almost identical to that of the bearish On-Neck Line except that the downtrend may

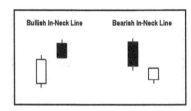

Figure 4.6 In-Neck Line.

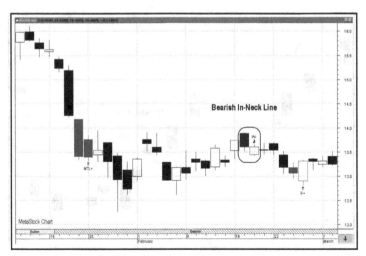

Figure 4.7 Bearish In-Neck Line–Alcoa, Inc., daily.
(METASTOCK WITH JCPR ADD-ON.)

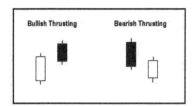

Figure 4-8 Thrusting Lines.

not continue quite as abruptly because of the somewhat higher close.

The daily chart of Alcoa, Inc (AA; Figure 4.7), shows an example of a bearish In-Neck Line. The formation of the In-Neck Line signaled that the sideways consolidation period was over and that another push lower was beginning.

The *Thrusting Line* (*CCE* 229–235) is another continuation pattern that is similar to the On-Neck Line and the In-Neck Line, but it closes deeper into the real body of the previous candle. The bearish Thrusting Line pattern is the third derivative of a failed Piercing Line because it does not close at or above the halfway mark of the previous candle's body. The bullish Thrusting Line pattern is not part of the original Japanese literature and was created as a complement to the bearish Thrusting Line pattern. Figure 4.8 shows an example of the Thrusting Line pattern.

The bearish Thrusting Line begins with a black day formed in a

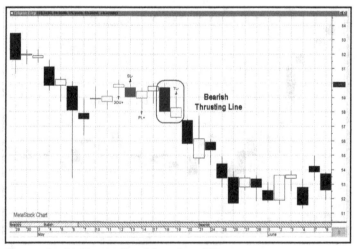

Figure 4.9 Bearish Thrusting Line–Celgene Corp. daily.
(METASTOCK WITH JCPR ADD-ON.)

downtrend. The second day is white and opens considerably lower than the low of the first day. The second day closes well into the body of the first day but not above the midpoint.

Much like the bearish On-Neck Line and the bearish In-Neck Line patterns, the bearish Thrusting Line represents a failure to rally in a down market. Because of this failure, the bulls will be discouraged, and a lack of buying will allow the downtrend to continue. The daily chart of Celgene Corp. (CELG; Figure 4.9) shows an example of a bearish Thrusting Line.

Additional Information on the On-Neck Line, In-Neck Line, and Thrusting Line Patterns

You may wonder why there are three continuation patterns that are derived from a failure to complete a Piercing Line. The bearish On-Neck Line, bearish In-Neck Line, and bearish Thrusting Line all represent failed attempts to reverse the downtrend. In the Japanese literature, there were no bullish counterparts for these for a failed Dark Cloud Cover. This is so because the bottoming process generally is more abrupt and pronounced, whereas the topping process can be a long, drawn-out affair.

THREE-DAY PATTERNS

The *Upside Tasuki Gap* and *Downside Tasuki Gap* (CCE 236–240) are formed when a gap that opened the previous day is not closed by an opposite-colored candle. An Upside *Tasuki* Gap is a white candlestick

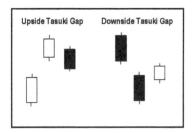

Figure 4.10 Tasuki Gaps.

that has gapped above the previous white candlestick and then is followed by a black candlestick that closes inside that gap. This last day also must open inside the second white day's body. An important point is that the gap made between the first two days is not filled. The philosophy is that one should go long on the close of the last day. The Downside *Tasuki* Gap uses the same concept, only reversed. Figure 4.10 shows examples of *Tasuki* Gaps.

The psychology of the *Tasuki* Gap is quite simple: Go with the trend of the gap. The correction day (the third day) did not fill the gap, and the trend should continue. This is looked on as temporary profit-taking.

The daily chart of Exxon Mobil Corp. (XOM; Figure 4.11) shows an example of an Upside *Tasuki* Gap. Price had been working its way higher prior to formation of the *Tasuki* Gap. The fact that the upside gap remained open drew buying interest from traders, who pushed the price of XOM higher over the next week.

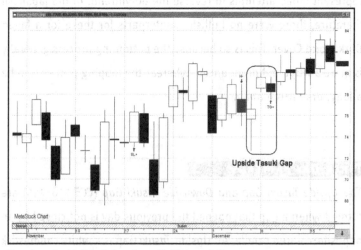

Figure 4.11 Upside Tasuki Gap–Exxon Mobil Corp. daily.
(METASTOCK WITH JCPR ADD-ON.)

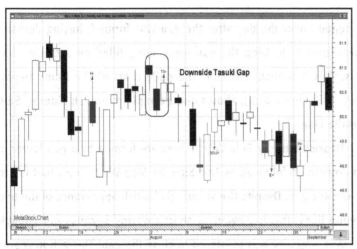

Figure 4.12 Downside Tasuki Gap—The Travelers Companies, Inc., daily.
(METASTOCK WITH JCPR ADD-ON.)

The daily chart of The Travelers Companies, Inc. (TRV; Figure 4.12), shows an example of a Downside *Tasuki* Gap. This bearish three-day pattern formed at the end of a corrective bounce, signaling that the push lower was ready to resume.

Side-by-Side White Lines (CCE 241–246) indicate a pause or stalemate when they are by themselves. The important aspect of this pattern is that two white lines have gapped in the direction of the current trend, and the subsequent two days were unable to close that gap. Figure 4.13 shows examples of Side-by-Side White Lines.

Bullish Side-by-Side White Lines are formed in an uptrend when two white candlesticks of similar size are side by side after gapping above another white candlestick. Not only are they of similar size, but the opening price should be very close. This pattern is psychologically important because even though the market

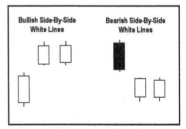

Figure 4.13 Side-by-Side White Lines.

opened lower the day after the gap was formed, buying demand was enough to keep the gap from being filled on a closing basis. This is bullish behavior. The daily chart of The Home Depot, Inc. (HD; Figure 4.14), shows and example of bullish Side-by-Side White Lines.

Bearish Side-by-Side White Lines are formed by a gap lower in a downtrend followed by two Side-By-Side White Lines that fail to close the gap. Despite the seemingly bullish appearance of the two white lines, this is viewed as short covering because not enough buying pressure was mustered to close the gap. This action represents the market taking a rest or buying time. It would be a normal expectation to have two Side-by-Side Black Lines for this continuation pattern. Two black lines following a gap lower would not be of much use, however, because they would represent obvious weakness in an already existing downtrend.

Figure 4.14 Bullish Side-by-Side White Lines—The Home Depot, Inc., daily.
(METASTOCK WITH JCPR ADD-ON.)

The daily chart of Global Payments, Inc. (GPN; Figure 4.15), shows an example of bearish Side-by-Side White Lines. Even though the pattern shown resembles two straight Hammer patterns that could signal indecision and a possible change in trend, *the important point here is that the gap that was opened between the first and second candles remained open after completion of the third candle.* Remember, the gap here is between the real bodies, not the entire candles. The black candle formed on the fourth day showed that the downtrend had resumed.

The *Upside Gap Three Methods* and *Downside Gap Three Methods* patterns (*CCE 254–258*) are simplistic patterns that resemble the Upside and Downside *Tasuki* Gaps that occur in a strongly trending market. A gap appears between two candlesticks of the same color. This color should reflect the trend of the market. The third day opens within the body of the second candlestick and then closes within the body of the first candlestick (bridging the first and second candles),

Figure 4.15 Bearish Side-by-Side White Lines—Global Payments, Inc., daily.
(METASTOCK WITH JCPR ADD-ON.)

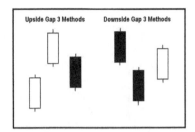

Figure 4.16 Upside Gap Three Methods and Downside Gap Three Methods.

which would make it the opposite color of the first two days. This would close the gap. Figure 4.16 shows examples of the Upside Gap Three Methods and the Downside Gap Three Methods.

This pattern forms in a market that is moving strongly in one direction. The move is extended further by another day that gaps even more in the direction of the trend. The third day opens well into the body of the second day and then completely fills the gap. The gap-closing move should be looked on as supportive of the current trend. Gaps normally provide excellent support and/or resistance points when considered after a reasonable period of time. Because this gap is filled within one day, some other considerations should be made. If this is the first gap of a move, then the reaction (third day) can be considered as profit-taking.

The daily chart of Rackspace Hosing, Inc. (RAX; Figure 4.17), shows an example of an Upside Gap Three Methods pattern. Notice how

Figure 4.17 Upside Gap Three Methods–Rackspace Hosting, Inc., daily.
(METASTOCK WITH JCPR ADD-ON.)

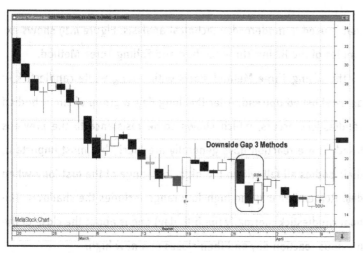

Figure 4.18 Downside Gap three Methods—Quest Software, Inc., Daily.
(METASTOCK WITH JCPR ADD-ON.)

price continued a mild pullback after the gap was filled, but the up-trend quickly resumed.

The daily chart of Quest Software, Inc. (QSFT; Figure 4.18), shows an example of a Downside Gap Three Methods pattern. Notice how Quest had been in a strong month-long downtrend. The Downside Gap Three Methods pattern gave way to one more push lower before price reversed higher.

FOUR-DAY OR MORE PATTERNS

The *Rising Three Method* and *Falling Three Method* (CCE 262–267) represent breaks in the trend without causing a reversal. They are days of rest in the market action and can be used to add to existing positions. These patterns are very similar to the Gann Pullback pattern

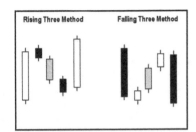

Figure 4.19 Rising Three Method and Falling Three Method.

that is used in modern-day technical analysis. Figure 4.19 shows examples of the Rising Three Method and Falling Three Method.

The Rising Three Method starts with a long white candlestick in an established uptrend. After this long day, a group of small-bodied candlesticks occurs, which shows some resistance to the previous trend. These reaction days generally are black, but most important, their bodies all fall within the high-low range of the first long white day. Remember that the high-low range includes the shadows. The final candlestick (normally the fifth day) opens above the close of the previous reaction day and then closes at a new high.

According to ancient Japanese literature, this pattern represents a rest from battle. If you think about it, trading in today's market is a battle every day, so this analogy really does make sense. In more modern terms, we would just say that the trend is taking a break before resuming its climb.

Bearishness tends to build over the three-day pullback period as the lengths of the candles increase, but the bulls eventually return to the market once they see that a new low cannot be made after the third reaction day.

The daily chart of Exxon Mobil Corp. (XOM; Figure 4.20) shows an example of a Rising Three Method. Even though this pattern does not quite match the "textbook" illustration above, the basic concept of the pattern is still intact. A white candle in an uptrend is followed by three straight candles within the daily range of that candle. The uptrend then resumes with a long white candle exploding out of the three-day consolidation.

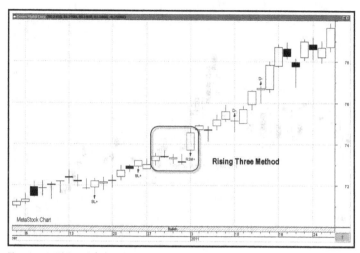

Figure 4.20 Rising Three Method–Exxon Mobil Corp. daily.
(METASTOCK WITH JCPR ADD-ON.)

The Falling Three Method pattern is the bearish counterpart to the Rising Three Method pattern. A downtrend is underway, and it is further perpetuated with a long black candlestick. The next three days produce small-body days that move against the trend. It is best if the bodies of those reactionary days are white. It is noted that the bodies all remain within the high-low range of the first black candlestick. The last day should open near the previous day's close and then close at a new low. The market's rest is over.

The daily chart of Granite Construction, Inc. (GVA; Figure 4.21), shows an example of a Falling Three Method. Notice that the trend had been in place before formation of the pattern. Once the pattern concluded, the downtrend resumed.

The *Three-Line Strike* pattern (CCE 275–280) is a four-day pattern that appears in a defined trend. It can be looked on as an extended

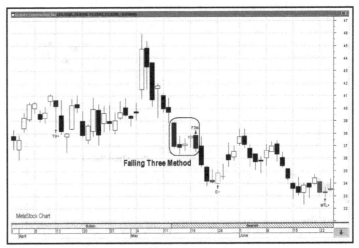

Figure 4.21 Falling Three Method–Granite Construction, Inc., daily.
(METASTOCK WITH JCPR ADD-ON.)

version of either the Three Black Crows pattern (bearish) or the Three White Soldiers pattern (bullish). This pattern is a resting or pausing pattern; the rest is accomplished in only one day. Breaks in the trend are almost always healthy for the trend. Figure 4.22 shows examples of the Three-Line Strike.

The bullish Three-Line Strike pattern consists of three white days with consecutively higher highs that are followed by a long black day. This long black day opens at a new high and then plummets to a lower low than the first white day of the pattern. This type of action completely erases the previous three-day upward march. If the previous trend was strong, this should be looked at as just a setback with some profit-taking. This last day is considered a liquidating day that will give the upward trend needed strength.

The daily chart of O'Reilly Automotive, Inc. (ORL; Figure 4.23), shows an example of a bullish Three-Line Strike pattern.

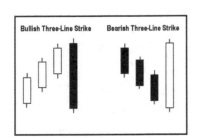

Figure 4.22 Three-Line Strike.

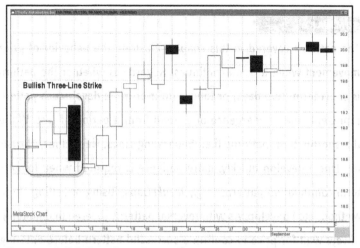

Figure 4.23 Bullish Three-Line Strike–O'Reilly Automotive, Inc., daily.
(METASTOCK.)

The bearish Three-Line Strike consists of three black days that each have consecutively lower lows. The fourth day opens at a new low and then rallies to close above the high of the first black day. This last long white day completely negated the previous three black days. This day should be looked on as a day when shorts were being covered, and the down move should continue.

A natural assumption that arises regarding this pattern is that if an Engulfing pattern is a reversal pattern for a single-day candle, then this surely must be a reversal pattern because gains from the previous *three* days were erased. Think of the Three-Line Strike pattern this way: This is an example of a market moving "too far, too fast," which means that some sort of reaction in the opposite direction is expected when either longs are washed out or shorts get squeezed. Only in this case the reaction to the Engulfing candle on the fourth day is a further push in the direction of an already existing trend.

SUMMARY

The patterns covered in this chapter illustrate the behavior of price movement when a trend continues. Regardless whether the pattern is short term (two days) or longer (four or more days), each pattern represents the reemergence of a trend from a period of rest. While the shorter-term patterns (i.e., Separating Lines, Neck Lines, Thrusting Lines) develop quickly, more patience is required when longer-term continuation patterns (e.g., *Tasuki* Gaps, Rising or Falling Three Method, etc.) develop. As with reversal patterns covered in Chapter 3, *always* wait for price to confirm a successful pattern before entering a trade. In this case, wait for the trend to resume before adding new positions. Mastering these patterns and the trader psychology behind them can help you to gain successful entry into a trend whether you either "missed the boat" as the trend was established or you simply want to add to your winning positions.

QUESTIONS

1. Which continuation pattern is *not* an undeveloped or failed Piercing Line reversal pattern?
   A. In-Neck Line
   B. On-Neck Line
   C. Separating Lines
   D. Thrusting Line

2. Which continuation pattern closes the farthest into the previous candle's real body?

   A. In-Neck Line

   B. On-Neck Line

   C. Separating Lines

   D. Thrusting Line

3. Which continuation pattern is similar to but the opposite of Meeting Lines?

   A. Separating Lines

   B. *Tasuki* Lines

   C. In-Neck Line

   D. On-Neck Line

4. Which continuation pattern closes at the extreme high or low of the previous day?

   A. On-Neck Line

   B. In-Neck Line

   C. Thrusting Line

   D. All the above

5. Which continuation pattern shows continuation of the trend with an unfilled gap?

   A. Upside Gap Three or Downside Gap Three Methods

   B. *Tasuki* Gap

   C. Side-by-Side White Lines

   D. Both B and C

6. What is a characteristic of the Rising or Falling Three Method?

   A. A gap must be left unfilled.

   B. A group of small-bodied candlesticks appears within the range of the first day.

   C. The second and third days must be Side-by-Side White Lines.

   D. Both A and C.

7. Which continuation pattern engulfs the previous three days?

   A. Upside/Downside Gap Three Methods

   B. Rising or Falling Three Method

   C. Three-Line Strike

   D. Engulfing Pattern

8. Which continuation pattern forms a gap in the direction of a trend that is immediately closed the next day?

   A. *Tasuki* Gap

   B. Side-by-Side White Lines

   C. Upside/Downside Gap Three Methods

   D. On-Neck Line

9. Which continuation pattern closes very near or equal to the previous day's close?

   A. In-Neck Line

   B. On-Neck Line

   C. Thrusting Line

   D. Nagasaki Neck Breaker

10. Which continuation pattern is defined as a gap that is opened the previous day that is not closed by a candle of the opposite color?

    A. Side-by-Side White Lines

    B. *Tasuki* Gap

    C. Upside/Downside Gap Three Methods

    D. Three-Line Strike

11. What is the name of the continuation pattern in the chart below?

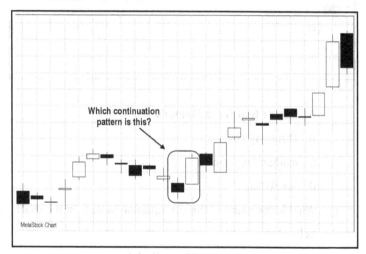

A. Meeting Lines

B. Separating Lines

C. On-Neck Line

D. In-Neck Line

12. What is the name of the continuation pattern in the chart below?

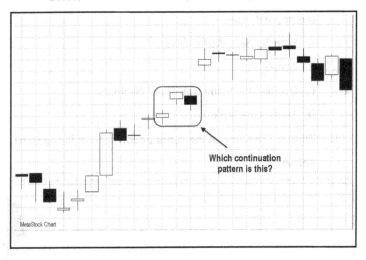

A. Upside Gap Three Methods

B. Thrusting Line

C. *Ichiban* Eruption

D. *Tasuki* Gap

13. What is the name of the continuation pattern in the chart below?

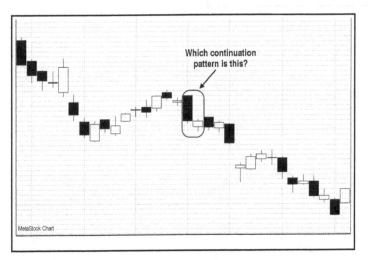

A. In-Neck Line

B. On-Neck Line

C. Thrusting Line

D. Separating Lines

14. What is the name of the continuation pattern in the chart below?

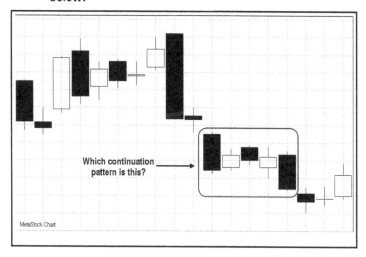

A. Downside Gap Three Methods

B. Three-Line Strike

C. Falling Three Method

D. Three Outside Down

15. What is the name of the continuation pattern in the chart below?

A. Piercing Line

B. On-Neck Line

C. Thrusting Line

D. Separating Lines

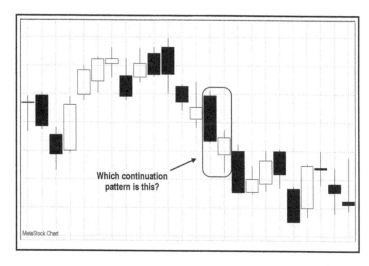

10. What is the name of the candlestick pattern in the chart below?

A. Downstairs Tasuki Three Methods

B. Three Inside Strike

C. Falling Three Method

D. Three Outside Down

11. What is the name of the continuation pattern in the chart below?

A. Piercing Line

B. On Neck Line

C. Thrusting Line

D. Separating Lines

5

INTELLIGENCE BRIEFING: PATTERN IDENTIFICATION AND FILTERING

In Chapters 2 through 4, I covered the basics of candlestick construction, reversal patterns, and continuation patterns. Throughout those chapters, I have shown how to use general rules to identify trends, long candles, short candles, and so on. This chapter will dig deeper into candle pattern recognition, which will eliminate needless speculation or doubt as to whether or not you are truly looking at an uptrend, downtrend, long candle, short candle, and so on. This knowledge will permit you to set up filters to allow for automated recognition of patterns through popular charting software such as MetaStock. Using a computer to recognize candlestick patterns can save a lot of time owing to the computer's ability to process and filter vast amounts of data. Statistics tell you the *odds* of something occurring, but they cannot predict with certainty *what actually will happen*. Even though the statistical results of scans and filters may look impressive, they cannot capture the most important element in trading—human psychology. Human psychology is best explained as the method by which traders react to the data *they* have processed, such as news stories, earnings reports, and so on. This always lends an element of unpredictability that a computer simply cannot capture. Let's step through the human element that is present each and every trading day.

In the first few minutes of the trading day, a great deal of overnight emotion is captured. Sometimes special events cause chaos. For example, on the New York Stock Exchange (NYSE) it may take several minutes for a specialist to open a stock for trading because of a large order imbalance. However, once a stock or commodity does open, a point of reference has been established. From this reference point, trading decisions are made throughout the day.

As the trading day progresses, extremes are reached as speculator emotion is tossed around. These extremes of emotion are recorded as the high and low of the trading day. Finally, the trading day ends, and the last trade is recorded as the closing price. This is the price that many will use to help make decisions about their positions and the tactics they will use at the open of the next trading day.

So how, through the daily ebb and flow of human emotion, does one determine the existence of a candlestick pattern?

Most candlestick patterns require the identification of not only the data relationship making the pattern but also the trend immediately preceding the pattern. The trend is what sets up the psychology of traders for the candle pattern to develop.

It must be stated here that Japanese candlestick analysis is short-term (one to seven days) analysis. Any patterns that give longer-term results are surely coincidental. This does not mean that longer-term price movements cannot begin from candlestick patterns, but the patterns themselves should be used only as short-term trade triggers.

Think of human psychology as the wild card that can trump even the soundest of trading preparation and analysis. When trading, the risk of human psychology is addressed through the use of stop-loss orders.

Some topics in this chapter also contain references to *Candlestick Charting Explained* in parenthesis (*CCE*) following the heading.

TREND DETERMINATION (CCE 306–308)

What is a trend? Technical analysis books deal with the subject of trend quite thoroughly and define it in a number of ways. One of the most common approaches is to use a *moving average,* which smooths the data being presented. A moving average is exactly the same as a regular average except that it "moves" because it is continuously updated as new data become available. When a moving average is rising, the trend is up (uptrend). Conversely, when a moving average is falling, the trend is down (downtrend). A close below a moving average in an uptrend or above a moving average in a downtrend may be a clue that the trend may be ready to change, but the main determinant of trend is the direction of the moving average itself. A moving average typically is computed using the closing prices of whatever time period being used. There are also many different types of moving averages used in market analysis, but the two most common are simple and exponential.

The *simple,* or *arithmetic, moving average* is the easiest to compute. To compute a simple 10-day moving average, add up all the closing prices over the last 10 days and divide by 10. A simple moving average gives equal weight to each of the closing prices, which means that the closing price 10 days ago means just as much in the calculation as today's closing price.

A somewhat more advanced smoothing technique is the *exponential moving average*. In principle, it accomplished the same thing as the simple moving average. Exponential smoothing was developed to assist in radar tracking and flight-path projection. A quicker projection of trend was needed with more influence from the recent data. The formula for exponential smoothing appears complex but is only another way of weighting the data components so that the most recent data receive the greatest weight. Even though only two data points are required to get an exponentially smoothed value, the more data used, the better. All the data are used and are a part of the new results.

An exponential average uses a smoothing constant that approximates the number of days for a simple moving average. This constant is multiplied by the difference between today's closing price and the previous day's moving-average value (these are the two data points needed). This new value then is added to the previous day's moving-average value. The smoothing constant is equivalent to $2/(n + 1)$, where n is the number of days used for a simple moving average.

After conducting numerous tests on vast amounts of data, a short-term exponential smoothing of the data was determined to best identify the short-term trend. It gives the best, easiest, and quickest determination of the short-term trend and certainly is a concept that one can understand. Simple concepts usually are more reliable and certainly more credible. The exponential period of 10 days seemed to work as well as any, especially when you recall that candlesticks have a short-term orientation.

IDENTIFYING THE CANDLE PATTERNS

Previous chapters presented detailed descriptions of the exact relationships among the open, high, low, and close. Those chapters dealt with the concepts of trend *use*, whereas this chapter focuses on trend *determination*. In addition, a method of determining long days, short days, *Doji* days, and so on is needed, including the relationship between the body and the shadows. The latter is essential for proper identification of patterns such as the Hanging Man and Hammer. The following sections will show the multitude of methods used to accomplish these and similar tasks.

Long Days (CCE 308–309)

Any of three different methods are available, and each or any combination of the three can be used to determine long days. The term *minimum* in these formulas refers to the minimum acceptable percentage for a long day. Any day whose body is greater than the minimum value will be considered a long day.

Long Body/Price – Minimum (1 to 100 Percent)

This method will relate the day in question with the actual value of the price of a stock or commodity. If the value is set at 5 percent and the price is at 100, then a long day will be any day whose range from open to close is 5 points or more. This method does not use any past data to determine a long day.

Long Body/High-to-Low Range – Minimum (0 to 100 Percent)

This method uses the body length in relation to the high-low range for a given day. If a candle does not have long shadows, it is considered a long day. Used by itself, this is not the best method, but used in conjunction with one of the other methods, it is good. This method will eliminate days that might appear more as Spinning Tops when viewed with the surrounding data.

Long Body/Average Body of Last x Days – Minimum (0 to 100 Percent)

An average of the body sizes of the last *x* days is used to determine a long body. The value for *x* should be anywhere between 5 and 10 days. If the percentage was set to 130, then a long day would be identified if it were 30 percent greater than this average. This method is good because it falls in line with the general concept of candlesticks and their use for short-term analysis.

Short Days (CCE 310)

The exact same concept used for determining long days is used for short days with one exception. Instead of minimum percentages, maximum percentages are used in these formulas.

Small-Body/Large-Body Relationship

The Engulfing pattern and *Harami* use both a large body and a small body for their patterns. This large-body/small-body concept is not the same as the long- and short-body concept discussed previously. Here, the large and small bodies refer only to their relationship with each other. You must decide how much engulfing constitutes an Engulfing pattern. If the concept is held to the letter of the law, then only one tick or minimum price movement is required to cause an engulfment. Can this be at just one end of the body when the prices are equal at the other end? In other words, can the open-to-close range be different for only one tick? The following formula will let you control the situation.

Small Body/Large Body – Maximum (0 – 100 Percent)

The inverse of this value can be used for the *Harami*. It is recommended to use values that represent what could easily be identified if the determination were made visually. If a small body is engulfed by a large body by 70 percent, this means that the small body cannot exceed 70 percent of the size of the large body. Said another way, the large body is approximately 30 percent larger than the small body.

Umbrella Days (CCE 310–311)

Remember, an umbrella day occurs when the body is at the upper end of the day's range, and the lower shadow is considerably longer than the body. You also must take into consideration the length of the upper shadow if one exists. The body and lower-shadow relationship is defined as a percentage of body length to lower-shadow length.

Umbrella Body/Lower Shadow (0 to 100 Percent)

If this value is set to 50, then the body cannot exceed 50 percent of the size of the lower shadow. In this example, the lower shadow would be at least twice the length of the body. The upper shadow on an umbrella day can be handled in a similar fashion.

Umbrella Upper Shadow/High-to-Low Range (0 to 100 Percemt)
The upper shadow is related to the entire day's range. A value of 10 percent means that the upper shadow is only 10 percent (or less) of the high-low range. These variables will help to identify the Hanging Man and Hammer candle patterns. Patterns such as the Shooting Star and Inverted Hammer use the inverse of these settings.

Doji Days (CCE 311)
Doji occurs when the open and close prices are equal. This is an exceptionally restrictive rule for most types of data and should have some leeway when identifying candle patterns. The formula lets you set a percentage difference between the two prices that will be acceptable.

Doji Body/High-to-Low Range – Maximum (0 to 100 Percent)
This value is a percentage maximum of the prices relative to the range of prices on the *Doji* day. A value in the neighborhood of 1 to 3 percent seems to work quite well.

Equal Values (CCE 312)
Equal values occur when prices are required to be equal. This is used for patterns such as Meeting Lines and Separating Lines. Meeting Lines require that the closing price of each day be equal, whereas Separating Lines require the opening prices to be equal. The same

concept used in determining a *Doji* day can be used here as well. There are a few instances where setting the parameters to the literal definition will restrict rather than enhance the pattern concept.

CANDLE PATTERN FILTERING (CCE 361–390)

Candle pattern filtering offers a method of trading with candlesticks that is complemented by other popular technical tools for analysis. Filtering is a concept that has been used in many other forms of technical analysis and is now a proven method with candle patterns.

Since any one indicator on its own can have inherent flaws, the synergy created by combining different methods of price-movement analysis can result in some very powerful combinations. When candle patterns are combined with other indicators, the results are superb.

The filtering concept was developed to assist the analyst in removing premature candle patterns or, for that matter, eliminate most of the early candle patterns. Since most technical analysts use more than one indicator to confirm their signals, why not do the same with candle patterns? Most indicators have a buy and sell definition to help in their interpretation and use. Most, if not all, indicators lag the market somewhat, however. This is so because the components of indicator construction are the underlying data themselves. If an indicator's parameters are set too tight, the result will be too many bad signals, or whipsaws. Therefore, a presignal area was determined based on thresholds and/or indicator values, whether positive or negative.

The *presignal area* is an area where a trader should look for some sort of signal that dictates that some sort of action should be taken, whether it is putting on a new trade or exiting an existing position. Statistically, it has been shown that the longer an indicator is in its presignal area, the better the actual buy or sell signal will be.

Each indicator has its own unique presignal area. When the indicator is in the buying presignal area, only bullish patterns are considered. Likewise, if an indicator is in the selling presignal area, only bearish patterns are considered. For threshold indicators, the presignal area is the area between the indicator and the thresholds, both above and below. Figure 5.1 shows an example of an indicator with upper and lower thresholds.

For oscillators, the presignal area is defined as the area after the oscillator crosses the zero line until it crosses the moving average or smoothing used to define the trading signals. Figure 5.2 shows an example of an oscillator generating signals.

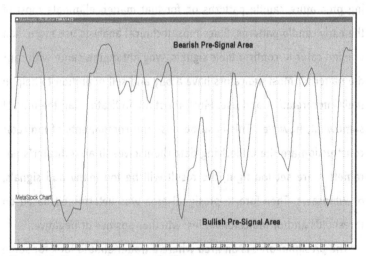

Figure 5.1 Indicator presignal buy and sell zones.
(METASTOCK.)

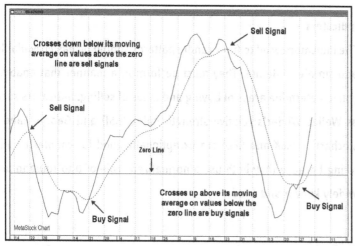

Figure 5.2 Oscillator buy and sell signals.
(METASTOCK.)

Chapter 9 in *Candlestick Charting Explained* goes into great detail regarding the backtesting of candle patterns with various momentum indicators. A wealth of statistical evidence is presented that shows how combining candle patterns with these indicators can enhance trading results. This chapter will present various momentum indicators, giving a brief discussion of each, along with a sample trade. It will be up to you to take your research and understanding of these indicators further to learn their characteristics and to develop a comfort level in using them.

Also notice the combination of candle pattern and indicator position in the trade setups. While these may seem like obvious hand-picked examples, you must realize that with the chart-scanning features in modern charting software, a user can scan for specific candle patterns and indicator positions to look for preferred trading setups. By making use of the technology available, any trader can filter setups to include only those that have a higher probability of success.

Indicators

The indicators used to filter candle patterns should be easily available and simple to define. They must perform in a manner that enables you to determine areas of buying and areas of selling. Indicators such as Welles Wilder's relative strength index (RSI) and George Lane's stochastics (%K and %D) are exceptionally good for candlestick filtering because they both use a normalized scale of 0 to 100 and are widely known and used.

Wilder's RSI

J. Welles Wilder developed the RSI in the late 1970s. It has been a popular indicator with many different interpretations. It is a simple measurement that expresses the relative strength of the current price movement from 1 to 100. Basically, it averages the up days and down days. Up and down days are determined by the day's close relative to the preceding day's close. Do not confuse Wilder's RSI with a relative strength measure that compares two securities.

The RSI at times does form classic chart patterns such as head and shoulders, but perhaps its most common use is for confirming or diverging from price movement. These divergences or nonconfirmations of price activity work well if the divergence takes place near the upper or lower regions of the indicator.

The default value for the number of periods used in the RSI calculation is 14 periods in many charting software packages. A setting of 9 periods is more common among commodity traders. If you can determine the dominant cycle of the data, that value would be a good period to use for RSI. The levels (or thresholds) for determining market turning points also can be moved. Using values of 65 and 35 seem to work better for stocks, whereas the original levels of 30 and 70 are better for futures.

Market trend also has an effect on where the RSI tends to top and bottom. For example, when using a 14-period RSI on equities, you will notice that the RSI tends to top at 70 or above and bottom at around 40 during uptrends. In downtrends, the RSI tends to top at 60 and bottom at around 30. Being aware of the trend in the market or security being analyzed can help you to determine the optimal presignal area to use.

The daily chart of Exxon Mobil Corp. (XOM; Figure 5.3) shows an example of the RSI diverging with price at or near threshold areas, which effectively warned of pending changes in price direction.

The RSI is a very effective tool for filtering candle patterns to look

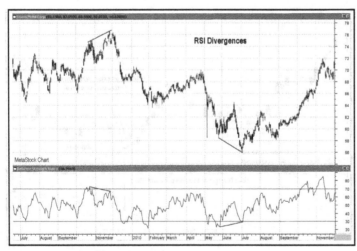

Figure 5.3 RSI Divergences—Exxon Mobil Corp. daily.
(METASTOCK.)

for the best trading setups. Of course, not every candle pattern results in a great trade, but using an indicator such as RSI with candlestick pattern identification can increase your odds of making successful trades. Once a valid candle pattern is identified and confirmed in conjunction with the RSI being in the presignal area, the candle pattern has more validity because a shift in price momentum is likely underway, thus giving the candle pattern more fuel.

Figure 5.4 zooms in on the July 2010 low in Exxon Mobil Corp. for a look at how combining candlestick pattern with the RSI can create good trading opportunities. In this example, we will label RSI values below 30 as being in the presignal buy area.

The first thing to notice is that the RSI broke down to its presignal buy area (below 30) twice in May 2010 (*circled*), but no trades would have been initiated. Why? Take a look at the candlestick patterns (or lack thereof) when the RSI dipped below 30. The first instance fea-

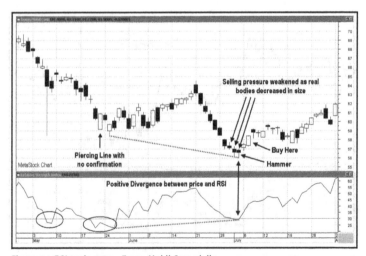

Figure 5.4 RSI trade setup–Exxon Mobil Corp. daily.
(METASTOCK.)

tured a black candle with a rather large body and a very long lower shadow. There was no upside action following that candle that would indicate that buyers were stepping up to reverse the decline. The second instance featured sloppy action as a combination of white and black candles chopped sideways with no discernible pattern to suggest that a meaningful reversal higher might be near. A bullish Piercing Line was formed on May 21, but there was no immediate confirmation to the upside, which made the pattern suspect.

The situation we will concentrate on is the reversal off the July 2, 2010, low. Here is how the trade setup developed:

1. The RSI showed a positive divergence with price because the RSI made a higher low in the presignal area and price made a lower low.

2. Selling pressure was weakening as the size of the real bodies of the last three black candles contracted.

3. A Hammer formed on July 2, showing that buyers were stepping up.

4. Price reversed higher on July 6 following the Hammer, forming the first white candle in 11 trading days.

Price continued higher the next day as a long white candle formed. A good place to buy would have been on the long white day when price broke above the high of the white candle formed on July 6. A protective stop should have been placed below the low of the July 2 Hammer.

Stochastic Oscillator %D

George Lane promoted stochastics many years ago. A *stochastic* is an oscillator that measures the relative position of the closing price within a price range over the last *x* periods. Just like the RSI, 14 periods is the default setting in most charting software packages.

Stochastics are based on the commonly accepted observation that closing prices tend to cluster near the day's high prices as an upward move gains strength and near the lows during a decline. For instance, when a trend is about to change from up to down, highs are often higher, but the closing price settles near the low. This makes the stochastic oscillator different from most oscillators, which are normalized representations of the relative strength or the difference between the close and a selected trend.

The calculation of %D is simply the three-period simple moving average of %K. It is customarily displayed directly over %K, making both of them almost impossible to see. Interpreting stochastics requires familiarity with the way they react in particular markets. The usual initial trading signal occurs when %D crosses the extreme bands (75 to 85 on the upside and 15 to 25 on the downside). The actual trading signal is not made until %K crosses %D. Even though the extreme zones help to ensure an adverse reaction of minimum size, the crossing of the two lines acts in a way similar to dual moving averages. One drawback to using the %K/%D crossover method as a trade trigger is that in strongly trending markets, premature crossovers can cause whipsaw signals. The trading example beginning in Figure 5.5 will use only a 14-day %D in the presignal buy area as the setup (below 20).

The daily chart of McDonald's Corp. shows the %D plotted in the window below price. The first thing to note is that %D never reached

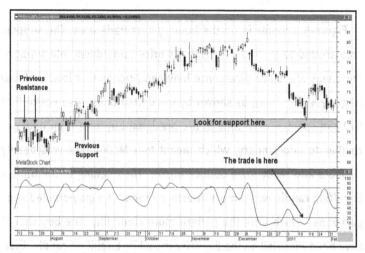

Figure 5.5 %D trade setup—McDonald's Corp. daily.
(METASTOCK.)

the buy presignal zone below 20 from mid-July through mid-December. This shows the strength of the uptrend.

On the price plot, there is a price zone around 72 that is shaded in gray. This is a support area that was formed by prior highs (labeled "Previous Resistance") in July and by support formed by consecutive lows prior to the beginning of the large advance (labeled "Previous Support"). Knowing older support and resistance areas on a price chart provides valuable information that can give a prepared trader an edge.

As in the RSI example, notice that the first time %D dipped into the presignal buy area (below 20), there were no valid candle patterns showing that a reversal higher was imminent. Whenever there are no clear signals, it is always best to stand aside until a clearer picture of price action develops.

Figure 5.6 zooms in on the January 2011 trade area. The support area around 72 is shaded in gray. As price came down into support, there was a positive divergence between price (lower low) and %D (slightly higher low), as shown by the dotted lines. Also notice that %D had spent a lot of time in the presignal buy area from mid-December to mid-January, which meant that McDonald's was deeply oversold and ready for a bounce higher. The opening of the bullish Engulfing candle was almost directly on top of the gray-shaded support zone, which gave the pattern more credibility. The buy should have been executed on the day after the white Engulfing candle. Even though the candle following the Engulfing candle was an unimpressive Spinning Top, a small rising window along with the close over the high of the Engulfing candle showed enough strength to confirm the reversal. A protective sell stop should have been placed below the low of the white Engulfing candle.

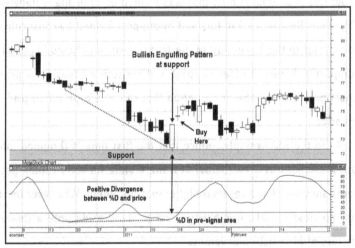

Figure 5.6 %D trade execution—McDonald's Corp. daily.
(METASTOCK.)

Whenever a position is taken following a deeply oversold condition such as this, you can expect a period of choppy price action as buyers and sellers battle for control. This was not a cherry-picked trade to demonstrate a rocket shot higher. This example was chosen to show the strength of a reversal pattern that forms at support. Even though the price action struggled for a time, the protective sell stop price was never close to being touched because price eventually worked its way higher. Also remember that candle patterns have a short-term effect (one to seven days).

The next example shows a 14-period %K (with 3-period smoothing) using 80 as the threshold level for the presignal sell area. The daily chart of Wal-Mart Stores, Inc., in Figure 5.7 shows an uptrend from December 2010 into mid-January 2011. As %K reached the presignal buy area, notice that a Spinning Top and a Hanging Man formed. This showed diminishing buying pressure. In this case, we

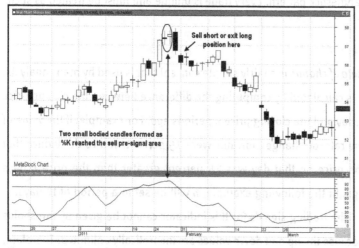

Figure 5.7 %K trade—Wal-Mart Stores, Inc., daily.
(METASTOCK.)

have an upward move that is running out of steam with %K over 80. This is a classic setup. Now all we need is a candlestick reversal pattern. On January 28, a bearish Engulfing pattern formed as a long black candle completely engulfed the real body of the Hanging Man. This was a signal for a more conservative trader to simply exit a long position or for a more aggressive trader to put on a short trade. For a short seller, a trade should have been placed the next day because price closed below the low of the Engulfing candle, which confirmed the reversal. A protective buy stop should have been placed above the high of the January 28 Engulfing candle.

Remember that %D is a smoothed version of %K, which means that %K is more active. This can increase the number of trade signals generated by %K, but it does not necessarily mean that the trade signals are any better. For every signal generated, a trader must take into account the trend, support and resistance levels, and the configuration of the candlestick pattern. Every trade is unique and must be treated as such.

Rate of Change

Rate of change is a fairly simple concept that is used by many analysts. It is calculated by computing the difference between the closing price today and the closing price *n* periods ago. For example, if the value of the rate-of-change indicator were 7.5 percent, you could deduce that the price on that day was 7.5 percent greater than the price *n* days ago. In the following example, *n* will be set to a period of 10 days.

The trading signals for this indicator cannot be given by thresholds because the up and down values are theoretically unlimited. Therefore, the trading signals are generated by the crossing of the indicator with its own 10-period smoothing. Ten periods for the smoothing value is used for most indicators that work this way. Better values may exist for certain stocks or commodities, but 10 seems to be consistently good.

Rate of change also has a center point or zero line that is used to show periods of positive or negative price momentum. Readings above zero are positive, which in our case means that the price is greater than it was 10 days ago, whereas readings below zero mean that price is lower than it was 10 days ago.

Rate of change also has the same ability as the RSI and stochastic indicators to show divergences with price. Even though there are no thresholds to use with this indicator, its position relative to price action can be very telling regarding the momentum or velocity behind price movement. The daily chart of Yahoo, Inc., in Figure 5.8 shows how the rate-of-change indicator is used with candlestick patterns.

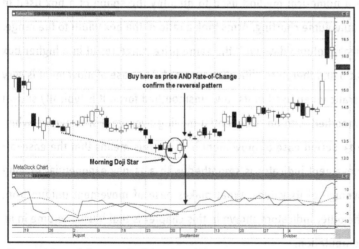

Figure 5.8 Rate-of-change trade—Yahoo, Inc., daily.
(METASTOCK.)

The trade was set up as price moved down toward what eventually would be an August 31, 2010, low. As price moved lower, the 10-day rate of change showed a positive divergence in the presignal buy area (*below the zero line*) by making a higher low (*dotted lines*). On August 31, a Morning *Doji* Star formed, with the *Doji* candle actually looking more like a Dragonfly *Doji* instead of a classic *Doji* Star. The price gap higher on September 1 completed the pattern because the rate of change barely crossed above its moving average. In order to be sure, a trade should have been placed on September 2 because the reversal pattern was confirmed with a higher close and the rate of change clearly moved above its 10-day moving average. A protective sell stop order should have been placed below the low of the *Doji* candle.

Ease of Movement

The *ease-of-movement* indicator was developed by Richard Arms. It is a numerical method used to quantify the shape of a box used in equivolume charting. Arms took a ratio of the box width to the range. Heavy volume days with the same price range result in a higher box ratio and therefore difficult movement. The ease of movement is very erratic when used in its raw, unsmoothed form. It is typically shown smoothed with an exponential moving average. For example, when a 13-period ease of movement is used, this means that the ease-of-movement indicator is smoothed with a 13-day exponential moving average of its values. What makes ease of movement unique from the other indicators shown in this chapter is that it uses volume in its computation.

The daily chart of Intel Corp. in Figure 5.9 has a 13-period ease-of-movement indicator plotted in the bottom window with its own 10-period simple moving average to generate trading signals as the ease-of-movement indicator crosses above and below the 10-day moving average.

The trade setup occurred as price declined throughout June 2010 into what turned out to be the July 2010 low. As price declined into the low, notice how the ease-of-movement indicator was in the presignal buy area and formed a positive divergence with price as it made a higher low and price made a lower low. As price continued its decline, a Spinning Top formed on July 1, followed by a *Doji* on July 2. The candle pattern and the ease-of-movement indicator both gave hints that downward selling pressure was waning. Price gapped slightly higher on July 6 as the high of the *Doji* candle was taken out. This price action, along with the ease-of-movement indicator crossing above its own 10-

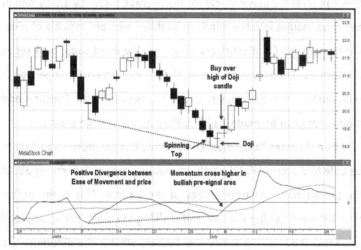

Figure 5.9 Ease-of-movement trade—Intel Corp. daily.
(METASTOCK.)

day simple moving average, gave a solid buy signal. A protective sell stop order should have been placed below the low of the *Doji* candle.

When trading with indicators, it is important to mention that indicators *reflect* what price is doing; they do not *dictate* what price will do next. It is easy for new traders to become enamored with indicators and the whole new world they can open up regarding the analysis of price movement. Indicators should be used as guides and nothing more. They can tell a trader when the ground is fertile for candlestick reversal or continuation patterns to be successful, but there is no guarantee that price will move in the direction the trader envisions, no matter how astute the analysis.

UNDERSTANDING THE MESSAGE

While candlestick charts are not needed for a person to trade well, they can level the playing field for the average trader by giving him or her extra insight into the mind-set of those who are capable of moving the market. Candlestick charting uses the exact same data set as Western bar charts, but by highlighting the all-important open/close relationship on a daily basis, subtle changes in trend direction and momentum can be made visible before actual change occurs.

When it comes to candlestick patterns, it is far more important to be able to discern what the pattern means instead of worrying about the proper name or terminology of the pattern. This is the difference between talking the talk and walking the walk. For example, if you know that a rising window is bullish, what is the difference if a bullish continuation pattern following the rising window is called a *Tasuki* Gap or a *Suzuki* Gap? Knowing the *meaning* behind a candle pattern will serve a trader better than reaching for a textbook to get the proper name of the pattern.

As was stated in Chapters 3 and 4, candle patterns derive their meaning from their position in relation to the trend and support/resistance levels. If a bullish Engulfing pattern forms in an uptrend, this is not a trend reversal pattern because the trend is already up. If a Dark Cloud Cover forms in a downtrend, it has no importance as a reversal pattern. Bearish reversal patterns formed at resistance have a better change of success than a bearish reversal pattern formed at support. A bullish continuation pattern formed at support has a better chance of success than a bullish continuation pattern at resistance.

The message of every pattern builds off the message of each day, which is made up of a body (the difference between the open and the close) and shadows (the high and the low). The real bodies take priority over the tails for the first read when evaluating and interpreting the candle message.

The body signal represents the sentiment of the day—the overall disposition after the smoke clears. Was the body small, normal, or large? Was it bullish or bearish, and if so, how bullish or bearish? The final score of a game determines a winner or loser, but the score does not always tell the complete story of the game. The trading day is the same way. For example, a bullish trader may finish the day with a small loss, but what was the action like during the day? Where did price close in relation to its open, high, and low for the day?

The tails (or shadows) represent the volatility of the day and confirm how hard it was to reach a consensus. Long tails can be news-related or just a result of lack of cohesion among traders, but they suggest a wide divergence of opinion and emotion. Shorter tails confirm and support the message of the body. Either way, tails increase or decrease the volatility of the day's action and reveal a lot about how the day's sentiment was reached.

Gaps are pricing phenomena that can have important implications. A true gap (with no part of the candles overlapping) is a rare and significant event that often accompanies strong price moves. A gap sometimes can punctuate a reversal because it signals strong sentiment as traders react to a stimulus of some sort, whether from a news story, an earnings report, or whatever. Gaps can be a complex topic because they can be categorized and labeled based on where they appear in trends. Regardless of how they are labeled, they all have the following traits in common:

1. A gap represents a sharp change in emotion regarding the price while the market has been closed. The opening price is higher or lower than the previous day's close.

2. The longer the gap stays open, the more significant it is.

3. Gaps happen a lot, and only rarely are they open at the end of the day.

4. How a gap is filled can help you to read the sentiment of the market.

Over 90 percent of gaps are filled by the end of the trading day. Therefore, an opening gap almost always will fill, and how it fills is important. If the candle reaches back to fill the gap and then continues on in the direction of the gap, the message is confirmatory of the gap direction. If a candle trades back to fill a gap and closes near or inside the previous day's close, it is often a reversal signal. The gap is a change in valuation, and how traders react is key to understanding how significant the gap is.

The daily chart of FedEx Corp. in Figure 5.10 shows an example of different types of gaps. The gap lower off the mid-February 2011 high (*gray-shaded area*) formed solid resistance to price advances over the next four months because the gap was not closed until July. This was a significant gap because rally attempts in April and May were turned back by the resistance area formed by the gap.

The second gap example was formed in mid-May (*gray-shaded area*) as price broke lower out of a consolidation pattern. Notice that the gap was filled first by a long white candle but then was reversed the very next day as a long black candle completely engulfed

Figure 5.10 Gaps—FedEx Corp. daily.
(MetaStock.)

the long white candle. This showed that the trend was still down.

The final two gap examples in June (again, *gray-shaded areas*) show what is known in Western technical analysis as *breakaway gaps*. These gaps show an acceleration of positive sentiment toward the stock because the gaps formed as price accelerated higher off the June 10 low. The driving forces behind these gaps were a positive earnings report along with an analyst upgrade that got traders excited about owning FedEx. These gaps have yet to be filled. Also notice that the move started by these gaps was strong enough to fill the February gap that had formed resistance for over four months.

Candle pattern analysis always should be used with other confirming techniques, such as the filtering techniques shown earlier or in conjunction with support and resistance areas. Filtered candle patterns consistently outperform a host of technical indicators and usually candle patterns by themselves. The combination of technical indicators and techniques is not new; in fact, it is the method of analysis most successful traders use. Adding candle patterns to the arsenal surely will improve trading results further.

QUESTIONS

1. How is a trend identified using a moving average?
   A. By the number of closes above or below the moving average
   B. By the direction of the moving average (rising or falling)
   C. By the number of times price crosses the moving average
   D. None of the above

2. Which moving average works best with Japanese candle-sticks?

    A. Short-term simple moving average (10 days)

    B. Long-term simple moving average (100 days)

    C. Short-term exponential moving average (10 days)

    D. Long-term exponential moving average (100 days)

3. Which method for determining a long day does *not* use past data?

    A. Price–minimum

    B. High-to-low range–minimum

    C. Average body of last *x* days–minimum

    D. None of the above

4. Which of the following statements is *true* regarding how to determine a small body?

    A. By its size relative to the previous 10 candles

    B. By the length of its shadows

    C. By its proximity to the moving average

    D. By its relationship with the previous large-body candle

5. Which of the following best describes the method used to determine an umbrella day?

    A. The length of the upper or lower shadow in relation to its daily range

    B. The length of the upper or lower shadow in relation to the real body

    C. The length of real body in relation to the previous candle

    D. Both A and B

6. What is the one wild card that can trump even the soundest trading analysis?

    A. Unexpected candle patterns

    B. Statistical anomalies

    C. Human emotion

    D. None of the above

7. What sets up the psychology of traders for candle patterns to develop?

    A. The trend

    B. Volume

    C. Long candles

    D. Short candles

8. Japanese candlestick analysis covers

    A. the long term.

    B. the intermediate term.

    C. the short term.

    D. All the above

9. What is the purpose of candle pattern filtering?

    A. To find trades that are guaranteed to be successful

    B. To create a synergy by combining different methods of price-movement analysis

    C. To eliminate most of the early candle patterns

    D. Both B and C

10. When an indicator is in the bullish presignal area,

    A. only long trades are considered.

    B. only short trades are considered.

    C. any trade can be considered.

    D. only swing trades are considered.

11. Using a 14-period %D stochastic with threshold values of 80 and 20, the area over 80 is called the

    A. bullish presignal area.

    B. continuation presignal area.

    C. strong presignal area.

    D. bearish presignal area.

12. When using a 14 period RSI,

    A. the RSI tends to top at or above 70 and bottom around 40 in uptrends.

    B. the RSI tends to top at 60 and bottom at 30 or lower in downtrends.

    C. the RSI does not exhibit any trending characteristics.

    D. Both A and B.

13. Which of the following indicators is good at showing divergences with price?

    A. RSI

    B. Rate of change

    C. Ease of movement

    D. All the above

14. Which of the following patterns has a *lower* chance of success?

    A. A bullish continuation pattern near resistance

    B. A bearish continuation pattern near resistance

    C. A bearish reversal pattern near resistance

    D. A bullish reversal pattern near support

15. Which one of the following candle patterns would be considered a solid trade setup with an indicator in the bearish presignal area?

    A. Three White Soldiers

    B. Growling Grizzly Bear

    C. Dark Cloud Cover

    D. Morning *Doji* Star

16. What is the theory behind stochastics?

    A. Closing prices tend to cluster near the day's high during an upward move.

    B. Closing prices tend to cluster near the day's low during a downward move.

    C. Closing price are random and show no pattern.

    D. Both A and B.

17. If %*D* is in the bullish presignal area and there is no bullish reversal candle pattern present, one should

    A. trade it anyway because momentum is in a bullish position.

    B. initiate half a full position and wait for a candle pattern to develop.

    C. do nothing—wait for the next opportunity.

    D. None of the above

18. Which of the following indicators uses volume in its computation?

    A. Ease of movement

    B. RSI

C. Stochastics

D. Rate of change

19. What is the purpose of using an indicator with candle pattern analysis?

A. To guarantee that price will move in the desired direction

B. To alert a trader when a candle pattern is likely to be successful

C. To determine what price *will* do

D. Both A and C

20. When using candle patterns, it is important to

A. make sure that the pattern is termed correctly.

B. be able to discern what the pattern means.

C. be aware of the trend direction leading up to the pattern.

D. Both B and C.

21. A candle pattern derives its meaning from its position in relation to

A. support levels.

B. resistance levels.

C. the trend.

D. all the above.

22. What should be the first read when evaluating a candle pattern?

A. The bodies

B. The tails

C. The pattern name

D. The pattern classification

23. What do the candle tails tell us?

    A. The volatility of the day

    B. How hard it was for traders to reach a consensus

    C. Whether buyers or sellers won the day

    D. Both A and B

24. Which of the following statements best describes gaps?

    A. They are almost always open at the end of the day.

    B. The longer a gap stays open, the more significant it is.

    C. Gaps occur rarely.

    D. Both A and C.

25. Candle pattern analysis always should be used

    A. on its own.

    B. with other indicators.

    C. only when volatility is high.

    D. only when volatility is low.

6

HONORABLE DISCHARGE: PUTTING IT ALL TOGETHER

The information herein was originally from a software product called *Greg Morris' Japanese Candle Pattern Recognition* that I produced in conjunction with Thomson Reuter's MetaStock. While I do not want this to be a sales pitch for the product, I do want some of the information to be widely available to the public. I hope that you enjoy it because my sole goal is to enhance your educational experience in candlestick analysis.

PATTERN DETAIL INFORMATION

The following example is taken from my book, *Candlestick Charting Explained:*

Pattern Name	MTL+	Matching Low +		Type	R+		
Japanese Name		niten zoko / kenuki					
Trend Required		Yes	Confirmation	No			
Frequency (MDaysBP)		590	Frequent				
Pattern Statistics from 7275 Common Stocks with over 14.6 Million Days of Data							
Interval (Days)	1	2	3	4	5	6	7
% Winners	69	64	62	61	60	59	59
Avg. % Gain	3.63	4.71	5.42	5.98	6.64	6.98	7.37
% Losers	31	36	38	39	40	41	41
Avg. % Loss	-2.06	-3.42	-3.92	-4.39	-4.75	-5.13	-5.48
Net Profit / Net Loss	1.23	1.43	1.55	1.65	1.77	1.79	1.82

Each pattern (bullish + and bearish −) has an information box. This box contains the *Pattern name* and *Symbol*—with + for bullish and − for bearish. In this example, MTL+ is the symbol used in this MetaStock software:

Type: R = reversal, C = continuation

Japanese name: Romanized name

Trend required: Yes or No

Confirmation: Required, Suggested, or No

Note on confirmation: This was an attempt to identify candle patterns that universally fell into two categories, patterns that seemed to never work well, and patterns that seemed to always work well. Those which never seemed to work well need confirmation ("Required"). Those which seemed to work well all the time do not need confirmation ("No"). A third category was derived because some of those which were originally in the "Worked well" category still had a few statistics that were not good; therefore, they were placed in the "Suggested" category, meaning that confirmation is recommended.

Frequency (MDaysBP): This is the number of mean (average) days between patterns with a classification of Quite frequent, Frequent, Average, Rare, and Extremely rare.

Statistics for seven successive days of performance: % Winners, Avg. % Gain, % Losers, Avg. % Loss, and Net Profit/Net Loss per Trade. The Net Profit/Loss per Trade value is simply the average percent gain (or loss) for all trades. Because the New Profit/Loss per Trade is the average result for all trades (winning, breakeven, and losing trades), it can be a positive or negative number or even zero. If the Net Profit/ Loss per Trade value is positive, this means that the average trade produced a net profit. If the Net Profit/Loss per Trade value is negative, this means that the average trade produced a net loss.

The Net Profit/Loss per Trade value is the sum of all individual trade results divided by the number of trades. If all trades produced either a gain or a loss (i.e., there were no 0.00 trade results), then the Net Profit/Loss per Trade value also can be calculated as follows:

Net Profit/Loss per Trade = (% Winners × Avg. Win) + (% Losers × Avg. Loss)

Remember: A good candlestick pattern will have positive Net Profit/ Loss per Trade values across many time frames. Among those patterns producing a net profit per trade, the better patterns will be those with smaller Avg. Loss (100 − % Wins) values (i.e., a −3.00 percent average loss value is better than a −6.00 percent average loss value). Candlestick patterns are not perfect, so when a trade doesn't work out, you want a pattern whose losing trades produce lower average losses.

When Using Software, Sometimes a Pattern Is Identified But Changes Color

The computerized pattern-identification process begins with the oldest data loaded and moves forward from there. Many times a pattern such as a bullish Engulfing pattern is identified and then is followed by a day where the close is higher, which would be a Three Outside Up pattern. Both patterns are identified. Sometimes you might see a blue continuation pattern turn into a green bullish pattern. Both are still identified, just the coloring changes; it is the latter pattern that you should consider. The other instance of change is when the trend measure changes from bullish to bearish in the middle of a developing pattern, and then only the first part of the pattern will be shown.

A Clear Top (or Bottom) Was Made and There Was No Candle Pattern

Candle patterns are not to be traded solely by themselves. Expecting a candle pattern to identify every top and bottom will only lead to frustration. However, after you study a number of charts, you will see that they can be reliable guides when it comes to identifying higher-probability turning points in the market.

Candle Patterns Included in Greg Morris' Japanese Candle Pattern Recognition

Reversal Patterns (Chapter 2)

E+	Engulfing+	DC–	Dark Cloud Cover–
E–	Engulfing–	MS+	Morning Star+
H+	*Harami*+	ES–	Evening Star–
H–	*Harami*–	MDS+	Morning *Doji* Star+
HC+	*Harami* Cross+	EDS–	Evening *Doji* Star–
HC–	*Harami* Cross–	AB+	Abandoned Baby+
PL+	Piercing Line+	AB–	Abandoned Baby–

G2C–	Upside Gap Two Crows–		SKS+	Stick Sandwich+
ML+	Meeting Lines+		K+	Kicking+
ML–	Meeting Lines–		K–	Kicking–
U3R+	Unique Three River+		HP+	Homing Pigeon+
3WS+	Three White Soldiers+		LB+	Ladder Bottom+
D–	Deliberation–		MTL+	Matching Low+
AVB–	Advance Block–		DS+	*Doji* Star+
3BC–	Three Black Crows–		DS–	*Doji* Star–
B+	Breakaway+		3OU+	Three Outside Up+
2C–	Two Crows–		3OD–	Three Outside Down–
3SS+	Three Stars in the South+		3IU+	Three Inside Up+
CBS+	Concealing Baby Swallow+		3ID–	Three Inside Down–

Continuation Patterns (Chapter 3)

TG+	Upside Tasuki Gap+		3LS+	Three-Line Strike+
TG–	Downside Tasuki Gap–		3LS–	Three-Line Strike–
SS+	Side-by-Side White Lines+		G3M+	Upside Gap Three Methods+
SS–	Side-by-Side White Lines–		G3M–	Downside Gap Three Methods–
R3M+	Rising Three Methods+		ON–	On-Neck Line–
F3M–	Falling Three Methods–		IN–	In-Neck Line–
SL+	Separating Lines+		TL–	Thrusting Line–
SL–	Separating Lines–			

Pattern Breakdown

The concept behind pattern breakdown is fairly simple. If all the days of the pattern were combined into a single candlestick, would the

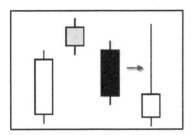

Figure 6.1 Candle pattern breakdown.

interpretation support the pattern or not? For example, Figure 6.1 shows the Evening Star pattern (bearish reversal) with the breakdown to the right of the arrow. The single candlestick line is known as a Shooting Star, which is also bearish. Therefore, the Evening Star breakdown is fully supportive and adds to the quality of the pattern. A number of patterns have breakdowns that are not supportive. Breakdowns that are supportive receive points, whereas those that are not supportive do not.

CANDLE PATTERN EXPERT

Note: This section discusses a feature that only exists in my MetaStock add-on product called *Greg Morris' Japanese Candle Pattern Recognition*. It is included in this book because it contains powerful information on candle pattern analysis.

Besides the automatic identification of candle patterns, the Expert Commentary is loaded with additional information to help you surmise the quality of the current candle pattern. An example of the Expert Commentary is shown in the following box. Below the example is an explanation of each section of the Expert Commentary.

GREG MORRIS' JAPANESE CANDLE PATTERN RECOGNITION

ANALYSIS OF: XYZ

Current close: 45.35

Trend is: Bullish

SUPPORT AND RESISTANCE LEVELS

SUPPORT	% FROM CLOSE	RESISTANCE	% FROM CLOSE
45.25	−0.10%	47.00	1.65%
43.12	−2.23%	47.35	2.00%
38.90	−6.45%	49.00	3.65%
35.34	−10.01%	54.80	9.45%

A Morning Star+ pattern was completed on 9/3/2010.

PATTERN SCORE	SCORE	MAXIMUM POSSIBLE	QUALIFIERS
Support/Resistance	25%	25%	−0.10%
Filtered	30%	40%	9%D,DI
Statistics	0%	15%	F
Volume	5%	15%	VL
Breakdown	5%	5%	Y

This pattern has a 65% chance of success.
Click here to see Pattern Information and Commentary.

Header, Close Price, and Trend

GREG MORRIS' JAPANESE CANDLE PATTERN RECOGNITION

ANALYSIS OF: **xyz**

Current close: 45.35

Trend is: Bullish

This information is available with each trading bar (I always suggest using daily bars) and is always part of the Expert Commentary. In this example, the stock being analyzed is XYZ, as shown above. The current close on the selected date is shown, followed by whether the trend analysis for this stock is bullish or bearish; in this case, it is bullish.

SUPPORT AND RESISTANCE LEVELS

SUPPORT	% FROM CLOSE	RESISTANCE	% FROM CLOSE
45.25	−0.10%	47.00	1.65%
43.12	−2.23%	47.35	2.00%
38.90	−6.45%	49.00	3.65%
35.34	−10.01%	54.80	9.45%

The support and resistance levels are calculated automatically by this product. In most cases, four support and four resistance levels will be identified. Sometimes, but not often, there will be fewer levels shown owing to sideways or range-bound trading in the prior few months. Support and resistance lines only appear in the Expert Commentary based on the last close in the data loaded.

Pattern Name

If the last day of a pattern is selected (default) for the Expert Commentary, the Pattern Name section will display the name of any pattern that is selected.

A Morning Star+ pattern was completed on 9/3/2010.

Pattern Score

PATTERN SCORE	SCORE	MAXIMUM POSSIBLE	QUALIFIERS
Support/Resistance	25%	25%	−0.10%
Filtered	30%	40%	9%D, DI
Statistics	0%	15%	F
Volume	5%	15%	VL
Breakdown	5%	5%	Y
This pattern has a 65% chance of success			

The pattern scoring will appear *only* when there is a reversal candle pattern that has been completed on the last day of the data loaded. This section of the Expert Commentary will not appear on any other selected date in the data, even if a previously identified pattern is selected. This is so because the support and resistance calculations are accomplished *only* on the last part of the loaded data.

There are four columns of information in the pattern score data: "Pattern Score" lists the five different components that make up the pattern score (described below). "Score" is the percentage that is awarded when it meets the various components' criteria. "Maximum Possible" shows the fixed maximum that a component can contribute to the pattern score. "Qualifiers" is a list of the various subcomponents that contributed to the score. The following subsections describe each component of the pattern score.

Support/Resistance

If a pattern falls on the appropriate support (bullish reversal) or resistance (bearish reversal) line and any part of the data (within the high-low range of the entire pattern) is touching the line, then it receives 15 percent of the scoring. If the body of the pattern falls over the line, it receives the full 25 percent in the scaling.

Filtered

A filtered pattern is one that is supported by at least one, two, or three technical indicators:

9%D	9-period %D stochastic (>80 or <20)	20%
14%D	14-period %D stochastic (>80 or <20)	10%
DI	+DI > or < −DI (DI = directional Indicator)	10%

Please note that these indicators are used for both bullish and bearish reversal patterns. Therefore, the filtering component could be 0, 10, 20, 30, or 40 percent depending on which measures are met.

Statistics

Determination of the statistical computation is based on a weighted average of the Net Profit/Net Loss and Avg. % Loss using a combination of performance periods. Obviously, the performance based on the next day after the pattern is most important and hence carries most of the weight. Candle patterns only make short-term predictions about trend reversal and continuation, so if the price moves in that direction initially, the pattern did its job.

The various codes are assigned from A to H based on the weighted score of the two categories used.

A = 15% Top 25 percent of all statistics in both categories

B = 12% Top 25 percent in the Net Profit/Net Loss category

C = 9%   Top 25 percent in the Avg. % Loss category

D = 6%   Top 25 percent in the Net Profit/Net Loss category but bottom 25 percent in the Avg. % Loss

E = 3%   Not in the top 25 percent or bottom 25 percent in either category

F–H = 0% Bottom 25 percent in one or both categories

Volume

Volume support is important as the psychological evolution of a pattern unfolds. The percentages used are as follows:

VL = volume on the last day >
than the 15 day average of volume   5%

VI = volume increased on each day of the pattern   5%

VC = volume on last day > volume on other days   5%

If all the volume conditions were met, the contribution to the pattern score would be 15 percent. Possible scores are 0, 5, 10, or 15 percent.

Breakdown

The contribution to the pattern score is simple. If the breakdown supports the pattern (Y), then 5 percent is awarded. If the breakdown does not support the pattern (N), then 0 percent is the score.

SOME JAPANESE CANDLE PATTERNS DO NOT APPEAR

My goal with this software product was to include all the real Japanese candle patterns. When I was translating the Japanese literature, most of the patterns were discussed in general terms. Remember, there were no computers, and it was strictly a visual process. I had to interpret the discussion and convert it into computer code for identification. There are a handful of patterns that are extremely rare (detailed discussion is available in my book *Candlestick Charting Explained*) and do not appear unless you search through vast amounts of data. For example, the pattern Three Stars in the South+ appears so infrequently that I deem it as almost useless. There were only 35 occurrences in over 14.6 million days of data. Unique Three-River Bottom occurred only 36 times. However, it was included because it was a pattern that was discussed in one of the Japanese books. The experimental data were accomplished on a list of 7,275 common U.S. stocks that included large data histories that totaled over 14.6 million days of data. Remember, these are just statistics and all based on past data—their frequency could improve over time or get worse. You just need to be aware of the fact that they are rare and not be concerned if you don't see them often, if ever.

Thus, when you see one of these *extremely* rare patterns, what should you do? I suggest that you make a note of it but do not act on it. For reference purposes, I have included a list of rare patterns first:

PATTERN NAME	FREQUENCY
	(MEAN DAYS BETWEEN PATTERNS)
Concealing Baby Swallow+	59,109
Side-by-Side White Lines+	16,295
Side-by-Side White Lines−	47,557
Three-Line Strike−	17,402
Upside Gap Three Mehods+	21,598
Downside Gap Three Methods−	18,365
Upside Tasuki Gap+	18,839
Downside Tasuki Gap−	20,278
Stick Sandwich+	19,338
Three-Line Strike+	20,506
Ladder Bottom+	25,260
Two Crows−	34,679
Advance Block−	60,833
Abandoned Baby+	87,952
Abandoned Baby−	89,571
Breakaway+	97,333

Here is a list of *extremely* rare patterns:

PATTERN NAME	FREQUENCY
In-Neck Line–	239,344
Upside Gap Two Crows–	317,391
Unique Three-River Bottom+	405,556
Three Stars in the South+	417,143

GREG MORRIS' INDICATORS

The following indicators are included with this software product and are located in the MetaStock indicator file.

JCPR Candle Trend

The Japanese Candle Pattern Recognition (JCPR) Candle Trend is a new method of identifying short-term trends and is used in *Greg Morris' Japanese Candle Pattern Recognition* automatically. However, it is also provided so that you can use it anywhere in MetaStock for any other trend analysis you would like to do. You can change the input value to increase or decrease the trend measure. The default input is set at 15. If you wanted to look at longer-term trends, just increase the input value as appropriate. For example, you can set it at 50 to see longer trends similar to a 50-day average.

The JCPR Candle Trend indicator takes into consideration the true range of prices and expands or contracts based on those ranges to follow the trend adaptively.

JCPR Candle Support and Resistance

The JCPR Candle Support and Resistance indicator is the one used in this product to automatically calculate the support and resistance lines. The input value is set at 126 and is the number of periods (days) that it looks back in the data to calculate the lines. You can increase the look-back periods to expand the concept. Sometimes it will encompass more data and widen the support and resistance lines, but not always.

PERSONAL NOTE FROM GREG MORRIS

The JCPR Candle Trend is a new indicator I created that is a powerful trend measure of the market. While it is used within this product to identify trends, you have complete access to it and can change the number of periods if you wish to identify longer trends of data.

Likewise, the JCPR Support and Resistance Indicator can be used outside this add-on. I think you will find that horizontal support and resistance lines are much better than slanted ones.

The system tests that are included in this product are not password protected, so you can change the stop-loss function. Currently, it is set as follows: Once in a trade, if the price moves more than 3 percent below the highest high value set in the last 15 days, it is stopped and awaiting the next candle pattern. The opposite is for shorting. If the stop is not hit, then an opposing candle pattern will trigger the next trade.

System tests serve many purposes, but I will adamantly state here that trading solely on candle patterns is not wise. Use the system tests with caution.

APPENDIX A

OTHER JAPANESE CHARTING METHODS

There are many other charting methods that are purported to have originated in Japan. I am not going to cover them in this book because they are more than adequately covered in other books. However, I do want to point out one thing: A charting method known as *Kagi* has been widely disseminated as being a technique that originated in Japan and was unknown in the United States until recently. The information that follows was from *The Ticker and Investment Digest*, May 1910, a print publication that was written in the United States over 100 years ago.

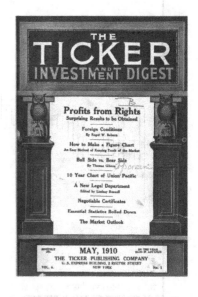

You can see from the cover page that the publication introduces a charting method known as a "Figure Chart." I honestly do not know if this type of chart was originally from Japan or not, but I do know it has been used in the United States for over 100 years. An example of the Dow Jones 20 Rails (now Transportation) taken from that publication follows:

I used MetaStock software from Thomson Reuters and recreated the following chart. As you can see, it is almost identical to the chart taken from the 100-year-old publication. The chart in MetaStock is called a *Kagi* chart because this is what many books on Japanese candlesticks call this method of charting. Personally, I don't think it originated in Japan, but I have no proof either way.

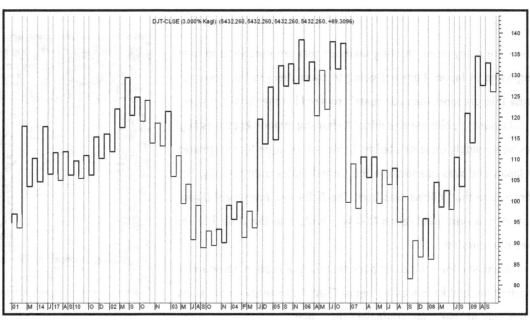

SOURCE: METASTOCK.

APPENDIX B

ACADEMIC PAPERS ON CANDLESTICKS

I have read many papers on candlesticks and, in particular, candle patterns. Below is a list of some of them if you want to further your study. I would suggest, however, that you treat them with a jaundiced eye because academics rarely get outside their sterile laboratory of modern finance ("Ivory Tower") and often take things out of context. An example is the identification of candle patterns and not considering the trend of the market at the time. This is just plain wrong in my opinion.

A good source for these papers and millions of others in the social sciences can be found at

Social Science Research Network
www.ssrn.com/

"Market Timing with Candlestick Technical Analysis," by Ben R. Marshall, Martin R. Young, and Lawrence C. Rose, Department of Finance, Banking & Property, Massey University College of Business.
Author's note: *The preceding paper includes my Three Outside Up/ Down and Three Inside Up/Down patterns. Clearly, we know which book these authors used for their research.*

"A Theoretical Foundation for Technical Analysis," by Gunduz Caginalp and Donald Balenovich, *Journal of Technical Analysis*, Winter–Spring 2003.

"The Predictive Power of Price Patterns," by G. Caginalp and H. Laurent, Mathematics Department, University of Pittsburgh, *Applied Mathematics Finance* 5:181–205, 1998.

"The Application of Japanese Candlestick Trading Strategies in Taiwan," by Yeong-Jia Goo, Dar-Hsin Chen, and Yi-Wei Chang, *Investment Management and Financial Innovations* 4(4): 49–79, 2007.

"Candlesticks and the Method of 3," by Gary S. Wagner and Bradley L. Matheny, *Technical Analysis of Stocks and Commodities* 10(3):121–124, 1992.

SOURCES

While I was in Japan in 1991, my friend Takehiro Hikita helped me to translate most of the following books. They were rich with market history, but my focus was on obtaining the various candle patterns and the details of their construction. Many cases were presented where the actual details were insufficient to develop the concept completely—keep in mind that much of this was done long before computers and basic technology were available. We strived to obtain patterns as close as possible with the information provided. Hikita-san had written about this a decade before, so his experience was invaluable.

Hikita, Takehiro. *Shin Shuu-Ashi Tohshi Hoh-Tohkel to Kakuritus de Toraeru* [*New Weekly Chart Method-Based on Statistics and Probability*]. IOM Research Publications, 1977.

Hikita, Takehiro. *Daizu no Sekai-Yunyu Daizu no Semekata Mohhekata* [*The World of Soybeans-Attacking Methods on Imported Soybeans and How to Profit from It*]. IOM Research Publications, 1978.

Kaburagi, Shigeru. *Sakimono Keisen-Sohba Okuno Hosomichi* [*Futures Charts-Explained in a Detailed Way to Be an Expert in Trading*]. Tokyo: Tohshi Nipoh Sha, 1991.

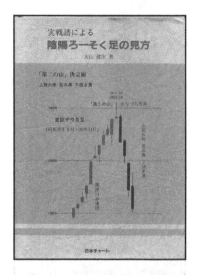

Kisamori, Kichitaro. *Kabushiki Keisen no Mikata Tsukaikata–Tohshika no Tameno Senryakuzu* [*How to Read and Apply Charts on Stocks–Strategies for the Investor*]. Tokyo: Toyo Keizai Shinpoh Sha, 1978.

Nison, Steve. *Japanese Candlesticks Charting Techniques*. New York: New York Institute of Finance, 1991.

Author's note: *Steve was one of the first to write about Japanese candlesticks and coined many of the translated names—I have not changed that.*

Ohyama, Kenji. *Inn-Yoh Rohsoku-Ashi no Mikata–Jissenfu ni Yoru* [*How to Read Black and White/Negative and Positive Candlefoot–In View of the Actual Record*]. Tokyo: Japan Chart Co., Ltd., 1986.

Analysis of Stock Price in Japan. Tokyo: Nippon Technical Analysis Association, 1988.

Sakata Goho wa Fuurin Kazan–Sohba Keisen no Gokui [*The Sakata Rules Are Wind, Forest, Fire, and Mountain*], 2nd and updated 3rd editions. Tokyo: Nihon Shohken Shimbun Sha, 1991.

Author's note: *The preceding reference was an excellent source for many of the candle patterns. The name* Fuurin Kazan *may be translated as "Fu–the speed like wind; Rin–that quietness like forest; Ku–that battle like fire; and Zan–that immobile position like mountains." This idiom originated from the Chinese battle strategy that Honma was said to have read.*

Shimizu, Seiki. *The Japanese Chart of Charts*. Tokyo: Tokyo Futures Trading Publishing Co., 1986.

Yasui, Taichi. *Kabushiki Keisen no Shinzui–Nichi Bei Keisen Bunseki no Subete* [*A Picture of the Stock Chart*]. Tokyo: Toyo Keizai Shinpoh Sha, 1981.

Yatsu, Toshikazu. *Tensai Shohbashi "Honma Shohkyu Hiden"—Kabu Hisshoh Jyutsu* [*A Genius Trader Sohkyu Honma into His Secret—To Be Confident of Victory on Stock Investments*]. Tokyo: Diamon Sha, 1990.

Yoshimi, Toshihihko. *Toshihiko Yoshimi no Chato Kyoshitsu* [*A Classroom on Charting*]. Tokyo: Japan Chart Co., Ltd., 1991.

CandlePower 6 Ultra Software

North Systems, Inc.

6821 Lemongrass Loop SE

Salem, OR 97306

503-364-3829

www.candlepower6.com

Authors Note: The CandlePower software is rich with candle pattern analysis, in fact, most of the statistics used in this book were generated by this software. If you are interested in detailed and accurate candle pattern analysis, I strongly recommend this software.

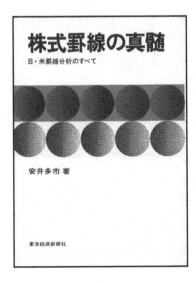

ANSWER KEY

1.	5. B	8. B
2. B		
	9. A	
4. A		5. B
	10. D	

9. A		
10. D		

CHAPTER 2

1. D	5. D	9. A
2. B	6. B	10. C
3. D	7. D	
4. A	8. D	

CHAPTER 3

1. C	11. C	21. C
2. A	12. D	22. D
3. D	13. A	23. D
4. B	14. C	24. C
5. B	15. D	25. D
6. C	16. B	26. B
7. D	17. B	27. B
8. D	18. D	28. D
9. C	19. B	29. B
10. D	20. A	30. D

CHAPTER 4

1. C	6. B	11. B
2. D	7. B	12. D
3. A	8. C	13. A
4. A	9. A	14. C
5. D	10. B	15. C

CHAPTER 5

1. B	18. A
2. C	19. B
3. A	20. D
4. D	21. D
5. D	22. A
6. C	23. D
7. A	24. B
8. C	25. B
9. D	
10. A	
11. D	
12. D	
13. D	
14. A	
15. C	
16. D	
17. C	

INDEX

(*f* following page numbers refers to figures)

Abandoned Baby pattern, 42, 42*f*
Advance Block pattern, 46–47, 46*f*, 47*f*
Arithmetic moving average, 99–100
Arms, Richard, 118

Bar charts, 120
Bearish Deliberation pattern, 49–50, 49*f*
Bearish presignal area, 7
Bearish reversal patterns:
 bullish reversal patterns vs., 8
 success of, 18
 (*See also specific patterns*)
Belt Hold line, 19–21, 20*f*, 21*f*, 74
Black Marubozu, 11
Breakaway gaps, 124
Breakaway pattern, 58–60, 59*f*
Bullish Deliberation pattern, 50
Bullish presignal area, 7
Bullish reversal patterns:
 bearish reversal patterns vs., 8
 success of, 18
 (*See also specific patterns*)

Candle pattern filtering, 105–120
 benefits of, 124
 development of, 7
 ease-of-movement indicator for, 118–120, 119*f*
 presignal area in, 105–106, 106*f*
 purpose of, 105
 rate of change for, 116–118, 117*f*
 relative strength index for, 108–111, 109*f*, 110*f*
 stochastic oscillator for, 111–116
Candle pattern recognition, 97–124
 filtering in (*see* Candle pattern filtering)
 identifying patterns in, 101–105, 133–134
 trend determination in, 98–101
 understanding the message with, 120–124
 uses of, 97
Candle pattern scoring, 139–140

Candle patterns:
   ideal, 7–8
   information in, 131–136
Candlestick charting:
   common mistakes with, 6
   history of, 9
   intraday and weekly use of, 5–6
   resources on, 149–150
Candlestick Charting Explained
   (Morris):
   continuation patterns in, 73
   reversal patterns in, 17–18
   statistics in, 4
Choppy markets, 18
Closing Marubozu, 11
Closing prices, 111–112, 137
Concealing Baby Swallow pattern,
   60–61, 60*f*
Continuation patterns:
   four-day or more, 85–89
   as market indicators, 73
   in pattern recognition software,
   135
   and reversal patterns, 8
   three-day, 79–85
   two-day, 74–79
   and waiting for price, 90
Counterattack Lines (*see* Meeting Lines)

Dark Cloud Cover pattern, 31–32, 31*f*,
   32*f*, 79

Data, 5–6, 9
Deliberation pattern, 48–49, 49*f*
Descent Block pattern, 47–48, 47*f*, 48*f*
Doji, 12–13, 12*f*
Doji days, 12, 104
Doji Star pattern, 32–33, 32*f*, 33*f*
Downside Gap Three Methods
   pattern, 83–85, 84*f*, 85*f*
Downside Tasuki Gap, 79–81, 81*f*
Downtrend, 99
Dragonfly *Doji*, 13, 13*f*
Ease-of-movement indicator, 118–120,
   119*f*
Engulfing pattern:
   Belt Hold line as, 21
   overview, 22–23, 22–24*f*
   and Three Outside patterns, 53,
   55
   and Three-Line Strike pattern,
   89
   use of small body and large
   body in, 102
Equal values, 104–105
Evening *Doji* Star pattern, 32, 32*f*, 33*f*,
   39–42, 41*f*
Evening Star pattern, 38–39, 38*f*, 40*f*,
   136
Exponential moving average, 6,
   100–101

Falling Three Method pattern, 85–87, 86*f*, 88*f*

"Figure Chart," 147

Filtered candle patterns, 140

Filtering techniques (*see* Candle pattern filtering)

Five-day reversal patterns, 58

Four-day continuation patterns, 85–89 (*See also specific patterns*)

Four-day reversal patterns, 58–62 (*See also specific patterns*)

Four-Price *Doji*, 13, 14*f*

Frequency (pattern information), 132

Gann Pullback pattern, 85

Gaps, 84, 122–124

Gravestone *Doji*, 13, 13*f*

Greg Morris' Japanese Candle Pattern Recognition (software):
    candle patterns in, 134–135
    Expert Commentary, 136–142
    indicators in, 144–145
    Japanese candle patterns in, 142–144
    pattern detail information in, 131

Hammer pattern, 18–19, 18*f*, 19*f* (*See also* Inverted Hammer pattern)

Hanging Man pattern, 18–19, 18*f*

Harami pattern, 23–27
    bearish, 25, 26*f*

bullish, 24, 25*f*

Harami Cross pattern, 26–27, 27*f*
    and Three Inside Down pattern, 53
    and Three Inside Up pattern, 51, 52
    and Three Outside patterns, 53, 55
    use of small body and large body in, 102

Header information, 137

Hi Ashi, 3 (*See also* Candlestick charting)

Hikita, Takehiro, 3–4

Homing Pigeon pattern, 34, 35, 35*f*

Human psychology, 97–99

Ideal candle patterns, 7–8

Identical Three Crows pattern, 57–58, 57*f*, 58*f*

Indecision, 10

In-Neck Line pattern, 77–79, 77*f*

Intraday data, 5–6

Inverted Hammer pattern, 27–28, 27*f*, 28*f* (*See also* Hammer pattern)

Japanese Candle Pattern Recognition (JCPR) Candle Support and Resistance, 145

Japanese Candle Pattern Recognition (JCPR) Candle Trend, 144

Japanese candlestick analysis, 9, 142–144 (*See also* Candlestick charting)

Japanese charting methods, 147–148

JCPR (Japanese Candle Pattern Recognition) Candle Support and Resistance, 145

JCPR (Japanese Candle Pattern Recognition) Candle Trend, 144

Kagi charts, 147–148

Kicking pattern, 36–38, 37*f*

Ladder Bottom pattern, 61–62, 61*f*

Lane, George, 108, 111

Long days (long candles):
    determination of, 101–102
    overview, 10, 10*f*

Long-Legged *Doji*, 13, 13*f*

Markets:
    as living entities, 1
    shifts in, 17
    uncertainty in, 14

Marubozu:
    Belt Hold line as, 19, 20
    in Concealing Baby Swallow pattern, 60
    overview, 10–12, 12*f*
    in Three Stars in the South pattern, 55

Matching Low pattern, 35, 36, 36*f*

Meeting Lines, 33–34, 34*f*, 104

MetaStock, 97, 131, 132, 147–148

Mistakes, common, 6

Morning *Doji* Star pattern, 32, 32*f*, 39, 40, 41*f*

Morning Star pattern, 38–39, 38*f*, 39*f*

Moving averages, 6, 99–100

New York Stock Exchange (NYSE), 45*f*, 98

NYSE (New York Stock Exchange), 45*f*, 98

One-day reversal patterns, 18–21 (*See also specific patterns*)

On-Neck Line pattern, 75–77, 76*f*, 79

Opening Marubozu, 11–12, 19

Oscillator:
    buy and sell signals, 106, 107*f*
    stochastic, 111–116

Panic selling, 57

Pattern recognition (*see* Candle pattern recognition)

Piercing Line pattern, 29–31, 30*f*, 75, 78

Presignal area, 105–106, 106*f*

Price data, 9

Price-based resistance, 6–7 (*See also* Resistance levels)

Price-based support, 6–7 (*See also* Support levels)

Rate of change, 116–118, 117*f*

Real body, 9–10, 10*f*

Relative strength index (RSI), 108–111, 109*f*, 110*f*

Resistance levels, 137, 138, 140

Reversal patterns, 17–63

    continuation patterns vs., 8

    four-day or more, 58–62

    identification of, 17

    as market shift indicator, 17

    one-day, 18–21

    in pattern recognition software, 134–135

    Stars in, 14

    three-day, 38–58

    two-day, 22–38

Rising Three Method pattern, 85–86, 86*f*, 87*f*

RSI (*see* Relative strength index)

Separating Lines, 74–75, 74*f*, 75*f*, 104

Shadows:

    message of, 122

    overview, 10, 10*f*

Shooting Star pattern, 27, 27*f*, 29, 29*f*

Short days (short candles):

    determination of, 102–103

    overview, 10–11, 11*f*

Side-by-Side Black Lines, 82

Side-by-Side White Lines, 81–83

Simple moving average, 99–100

Single-day candle patterns, 5 (*See also* One-day reversal patterns)

Smoothing techniques, 100

Software, charting, 4, 97, 133–134

Spinning Tops, 12, 12*f*

Stars:

    Doji Star pattern, 32–33, 32*f*, 33*f*

    overview, 14, 14*f*

Statistics, 4, 97, 132–133, 140–141

Stick Sandwich pattern, 56–57, 56*f*, 57*f*

Stochastic oscillator, 111–116

Supply and demand, 9

Support levels, 137, 138, 140

System tests, 145

Tails, 122

Tasuki Gaps, 79–81, 80*f*, 81*f*

Technical analysis, 86, 124

Three Black Crows pattern, 45, 45*f*, 46*f*

Three Inside Down pattern, 51–53, 51*f*, 52*f*

Three Inside patterns, 4

Three Inside Up pattern, 51–53, 51*f*, 52*f*

Three Outside Down pattern, 53–55, 53*f*, 54*f*

Three Outside patterns, 4

Three Outside Up pattern, 53–55, 53*f*, 54*f*

Three Stars in the South pattern,
    55–56, 55f, 56f
Three White Soldiers pattern, 44, 44f,
    45f
Three-day continuation patterns,
    79–85 (See also specific patterns)
Three-day reversal patterns, 38–58
    (See also specific patterns)
Three-Line Strike pattern, 87–89, 88f,
    89f
Thrusting Line pattern, 78–79, 78f
The Ticker and Investment Digest, 147
Trade entry, 73
Trend determination, 6, 98–101, 137
Trending markets:
    Belt Hold line in, 20
    and continuation patterns, 73
    Doji in, 12
    short days in, 11

Two Crows pattern, 50, 50f, 51f
Two-day continuation patterns, 74–79
    (See also specific patterns)
Two-day reversal patterns, 22–38 (See
    also specific patterns)

Umbrella days, 103–104
Upside Gap Three Methods pattern,
    83–85, 84f
Upside Gap Two Crows pattern,
    43–44, 43f
Upside Tasuki Gap, 79–80, 80f
Uptrends, 99

Volume support, 141–142

Weekly data, 5–6
White Marubozu, 11
Wilder, J. Welles, 108

ABOUT THE AUTHOR

Gregory L. Morris is senior vice president, chief technical analyst, and chairman of the investment committee for Stadion Money Management, Inc. In this capacity, Greg educates institutional and individual clients on the merits of technical analysis and why Stadion uses a technical rules-based model. Greg oversees the management of over $7 billion in assets in two mutual funds, separate accounts, and 401(k) plans. From December 2003 to May 2005, Greg served as a trustee and advisor to the MurphyMorris ETF Fund. He also served as Treasurer and chief executive officer of MurphyMorris Money Management Company, the advisor to the fund.

Greg has written his second book with McGraw-Hill: *The Complete Guide to Market Breadth Indicators*, a book introducing market breadth analysis for investors. A third edition (original edition in 1992) to his best-selling and vastly expanded *Candlestick Charting Explained* was released in March 2006.

From 1996 to 2002, Greg was chief executive officer of MurphyMorris, Inc., the leading provider of Web-based market analysis tools and commentary, with his partner, John Murphy, a former CNBC analyst. MurphyMorris, Inc., was acquired by StockCharts.com, Inc., in October 2002. In 1999, Greg and three associates started MurphyMorris Money Management Company to manage assets for individuals. This focus was later changed to address the firm becoming the advisor to the MurphyMorris ETF Fund in January 2004, and it later merged into the Stadion (PMFM) family of funds.

From 1994 to 1996, Greg was president of G. Morris Corporation, a Dallas, Texas-headquartered business that provided products and services for investors and traders. His lead product was a series of over 450 indicators and trading systems that supported most Windows-based technical analysis software packages. From 1993 to 1994, Greg was part of MarketArts, Inc., which launched the first Windows-based technical analysis software program, *Windows on Wall Street*.

In 1992, Greg published a book on Japanese candlestick analysis called *Can-*

dlePower, now available in soft cover as *Candlestick Charting Explained* (McGraw-Hill). Widely recognized as an expert on candlesticks and the developer of candlestick filtering, Greg has lectured around the world on the subject. From 1982 until 1993, Greg worked in association with N-Squared Computing, producing over 15 technical analysis and charting software titles, many of which are actively used today. In May 1989, Greg was awarded the Outstanding Alumni Award for 1989 by Pratt County College.

Greg graduated from the University of Texas at Austin in 1971, has a BS degree in aerospace engineering, has authored numerous investment-related articles, speaks at numerous seminars and investment groups, and has appeared many times on the Financial News Network (FNN), Fox Business, CNBC, and Bloomberg TV. Greg was featured in *Investor's Business Daily* in December 2007, *BusinessWeek* in July 2008, *Barron's* in January, 2009, *Stocks and Commodities* magazine in September 2009, and *Bloomberg Markets* in May 2011. Recently, Greg was invited to Italy, Brazil, Vietnam, Canada, Singapore, and China to lecture on the merits of technical market analysis. From 1971 to 1977, Greg was a Navy F-4 fighter pilot aboard the *USS Independence*, and he was selected for and graduated from the Navy Fighter Weapons School known as "Top Gun." Greg and his wife, Laura, live in the mountains of North Georgia.